CW00435083

Visitor
SAR

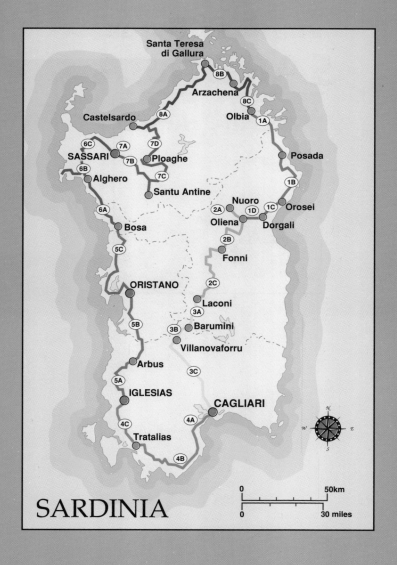

SARDINIA

VISITOR'S GUIDE
SARDINIA

Amanda Hinton

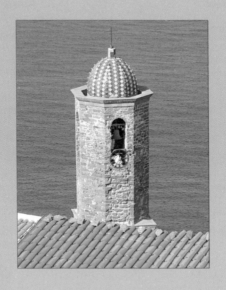

MPC

HUNTER

Published by:
Moorland Publishing Co Ltd,
Moor Farm Road West, Ashbourne,
Derbyshire DE6 1HD England

ISBN 0 86190 399 4

Published in the USA by:
Hunter Publishing Inc,
300 Raritan Center Parkway, CN 94, Edison, NJ 08818

ISBN 1 55650 596 5 (USA)

© Amanda Hinton 1993

All rights reserved. No part of this publication may be reproduced, stored
in a retrieval system, or transmitted in any form or by any means,
electronic, mechanical, photocopying, recording or other-wise without the
prior permission of Moorland Publishing Co Ltd.

British Library Cataloguing in Publication Data:
A catalogue record for this book is available from the British Library.

Colour origination by: P. & W. Graphics Pte Ltd, Singapore

Printed in Hong Kong by: Wing King Tong Co Ltd

Cover photograph: *Stintino* (International Photobank)
Rear cover: *Olbia harbour at sunrise* (A. Hinton)
Page 3: *Castelsardo Cathedral bell tower* (A. Hinton)

The following illustrations have been supplied by the Italian National
Tourist Office: pages 10,11,14,15,19,50,91,187; all the remainder by
Amanda Hinton

MPC Production Team:
Editorial: Tonya Monk
Design: Ashley Emery
Cartography: Alastair Morrison
Typesetting: Christine Haines

While every care has been taken to ensure that the information in this
book is as accurate as possible at the time of publication, the publisher
and authors accept no responsibility for any loss, injury or inconven-
ience sustained by anyone using this book.

CONTENTS

Key to Symbols Used in Text Margin and on Maps

🚶 Recommended walks		🛐 Ecclesiastical Site	
🦇 Caving		🏖 Beaches	
🏰 Castle/Fortification		⊼ Archaeological site	
🏛 Building of Interest		🖼 Museum/Art Gallery	
🌼 Garden		🔭 Beautiful view/Scenery, Natural phenomenon	
✳ Other place of interest		🐟 Aquatic Interest	
🐦 Birdlife		🌳 Parkland	
🦌 Nature reserve/Animal interest		⛵ Water Sports	

Key to Maps

═══ Dual Carriageway		⬤ City	
─── Main Road		⬤ Town /Village	
═══ Minor Road		River/Lake	
----- Provincial Boundary		------- Ferry Route	
─── Non Route Roads		✈ Airport	

How To Use This Guide

This MPC Visitor's Guide has been designed to be as easy to use as possible. Each chapter covers a region or itinerary in a natural progression which gives all the background information to help you enjoy your visit. MPC's distinctive margin symbols, the important places printed in bold, and a comprehensive index enable the reader to find the most interesting places to visit with ease. At the end of each chapter an Additional Information section gives specific details such as addresses and opening times, making this guide a complete sightseeing companion. At the back of the guide the Fact File, arranged in alphabetical order, gives practical information and useful tips to help you plan your holiday — before you go and while you are there. The maps of each region show the main towns, villages, roads and places of interest, but are not designed as route maps and motorists should always use a good recommended road atlas.

INTRODUCTION

Sardinia, renowned for its clear, blue seas, attracts 3 million tourists every year. Most come from mainland Italy to pass the national August holiday on one of the island's numerous fine beaches. The island as a whole is also popular with French, German and Swiss tourists, while British interest mainly focuses on the coastal resort of Alghero. The Sardinian coasts, which make up almost a quarter of the entire coastline of Italy, are undoubtedly the island's greatest asset. They offer enormous variety, from pink-tinged cliffs that hang over azure blue waters, to vast, gently-sloping, sandy beaches that are backed by dunes and scented *macchia* (Mediterranean scrub). There are beaches for scuba-divers, toddlers, trend-setters, or simply those that wish to get away from the crowd.

Sardinia also offers some exciting scenery inland. When D.H. Lawrence travelled through Sardinia in 1921, he was struck by the desolation, aridity and wide, open spaces. After having lived on the island of Sicily, he felt it was a place in which he could breathe. The visitor will undoubtedly be similarly impressed. The inland routes travel through parts of the country where only the jangling of sheep's bells break the silence of the landscape, and the occasional shepherd's croft is the only sign of habitation.

Sardinia is not, however, only a land of natural beauty. The Pisans and Genoans who ruled Sardinia around the twelfth century, endowed the island with some exemplary architecture. In the middle of seemingly nowhere, the visitor can come across a grand Pisan church, dramatically constructed in striped black and white stone, or intricately inlaid with geometric designs. The Spanish too left their mark on the island in the form of a chain of watch-towers lining the coasts and some graceful Catalan architecture in the towns. As well as this, the island is dotted with the remarkable, prehistoric remains of the Nuraghic era (circa 1800BC) which have left the interior pock-marked with robust towers, built of megalithic blocks of stone.

Last but not least, mention should be made of Sardinia's excellent food and wine. The island produces amongst the best *pecorino* cheese in Italy, as well as exquisite *ricotta* which is used in pasta fillings. Sardinian cuisine is based on shepherd's fare, which includes a wide selection of different types of breads. Amongst the most characteristic is *carasu*, which is wafer thin and crispy. It is also known as *carta di musica* after its resemblance to sheets of music. The sea-food found along the coasts is less traditionally Sardinian, as the Sardinians have tended, throughout history, to take refuge inland away from marauding, sea-borne invaders. It is nonetheless excellent, particularly the lobster and the *bottarga*, a Sardinian version of caviar, made from the eggs of tuna or mullet. For the wine-lover, there are the many interesting and individual wines, both red and white, which are made all over the island, some available through individual producers, others through cooperatives. The itineraries in this book pass through the most prestigious wine-making regions in Sardinia, namely Vernaccia, Vermentino, Mandrolisai, Cannonau and Malvasia, and in each of these regions the visitor will find *cantine* (wine-shops) where the local wine can be tasted and purchased.

The eight interconnecting routes in this book take in all of these many fascinating facets of Sardinia, travelling along the coasts, as well as through the interior. The itineraries are carefully planned so as to follow the most picturesque route from one place to the next, although more direct routes are also suggested for those in a hurry. The routes are divided into sections, each of which is well-packed with things to do and can be generally regarded as about 2 days worth of travelling.

History

THE NURAGHIC CULTURE
As far as archaeological evidence has revealed, the first inhabitants of Sardinia were prehistoric cave dwellers. By the neolithic era, however, the island's inhabitants had begun to cultivate the land and had even started trading. Archaeologists have discovered rock-hewn burial chambers, dating from the fourth millennium BC, and evidence that obsidian, from the extinct volcano of Monte Arci, near Oristano, was being exported at around the same time. However, the ethnic identity of neolithic man in Sardinia is, in reality, as vague as it is varied. In Gallura, there are ethnic similarities with the peoples of Liguria, which is on mainland Italy, around Genoa. On the south

coast of the island, it seems the inhabitants had cultural resemblances to the cultures of the West Mediterranean. While near Alghero, the Ozieri culture is attributed a euro-African ethnicity. Despite surviving architectural examples and well-preserved tools and implements, the early inhabitants of Sardinia appeared to have had no written language, and hence no documentation survives.

The era leading up to the Bronze Age, the dawn of the Nuraghic period, is similarly shrouded in mystery. The first half of the second millennium BC, which is when the earliest Nuraghic settlements are thought to have appeared, saw the arrival of a Libyan people, known as the Shardana. Little is known of the Shardana, except that in ancient Egyptian texts and cuneiform inscriptions, they are referred to as both enemies and mercenaries of the Pharoah. The coincidental timing of the Shardana and the Nuraghic people may or may not be significant. It is, however, increasingly widely believed, that there is some connection, since the Nuraghic culture has many similarities with Eastern Mediterranean civilisations. Perhaps the most striking evidence are the Nuraghic bronze statuettes, which bear strong resemblances to statues found in Egypt.

Again, the lack of written documentation leaves many unanswered questions, although there is a mass of archaeological evidence. The landscape of Sardinia is scattered with Nuraghic towers and the remnants of former Nuraghic settlements. These monuments are virtually unique to Sardinia, the only other place where similar constructions exist is in the Balearic islands, where there are far fewer. Seven thousand Nuraghic sites have so far been recorded in Sardinia. They are distributed throughout the island, with large concentrations in the fertile regions of Trexenta and Marmilla, and on the south-west coast around Sulcis, but above all they are concentrated in the north-west of the island on the high plains that lie between Oristano, Bosa, Nuoro and Oschiri, an area which was naturally easy to defend.

That defense was a fundamental concern, is clearly seen in the layout of Nuraghic settlements. A Nuraghic site is typically centred around a large, circular tower which is constructed of massive stones, without the use of mortar. The tower is generally of about 20m (65ft) in height and contains two or three floors. The walls of the tower are built in concentric circles, gradually getting smaller towards the roof, which is covered by a monolithic slab, forming a small platform. Spiralling ramps or staircases were constructed inside the enormously thick outer walls, connecting a room on each floor. The entrance to the tower was sealed from the inside, and was guarded by a niche to the right of it. Over time, the Nuraghic

A peaceful corner of Sardinia

(opposite) The azure blue waters of Sardinia's coast

Sardinia has inherited many remarkable prehistoric remains

settlements became more elaborate and more heavily defended, with the addition of defense towers and bastions. Sometimes, surrounding this fortress-type structure were the homes of the villagers. The village houses, also made of stone blocks without mortar, are typically circular and would have had dome-shaped roofs made of branches and reeds. In addition, solitary towers were built, two or three in a row, defending a vulnerable pass or an approach from the sea.

Villages also grew up independently of fortresses, particularly from 800BC to 500BC, the era of the Iron Age. Fifty villages dating from this period have so far been discovered. Most of the villages are made up of fifty to seventy circular, stone huts, with a central square and a nearby burial area. *Tombe dei Gigante*, as the burial areas are called today, have also been found separately from villages. There are 150 recorded so far, many of which are found in the high plains in the centre of the island. The tombs consist of a single, long and thin chamber where the people were collectively buried. The entrance to the chamber is often marked by a monolith with a very low door carved into its base.

PHOENICIANS, CARTHAGINIANS AND ROMANS

The Iron Age in Sardinia also saw the arrival of the peaceful, trading colonists, the Phoenicians. The earliest colonies were founded in the eighth-century BC. The Phoenicians exploited the island's natural resources, particularly lead, which they mined in the region around Sant'Antioco and exported from their colony at *Sulcis*. Important trading colonies also grew up around the natural harbours at *Karalis*, present-day Cagliari, and at *Nora*, which is one of the best remaining Phoenician sites on the island. From the sixth century BC onwards, the Carthaginians repeatedly attacked the shores of Sardinia. They gradually infiltrated the island, taking over the Phoenician sites, although failing to penetrate the interior, where the indigenous Sards, including Nuraghic descendants, were to resist invasion for centuries to follow. The fertile plains of Sardinia, however, were cultivated with grain, olives and vines, all of which supplied the city of Carthage, in present-day Tunisia.

The next stage in Sardinia's history was a by-product of the Punic Wars that were fought between Rome and Carthage. The Romans gained their first foothold on the island at the time of the First Punic War, in 238BC. Less than a decade later, Sardinia was officially announced a province of Rome, a status that was to remain unchanged for the next seven centuries. By 177BC, the only area of

Sardinia that was not under Roman control was the centre, which the Romans named *Barbaria*, after the war-like people, namely the indigenous Sards and Nuraghic tribes, that resisted them.

Like Carthage, Rome made use of Sardinia's natural resources. Along with Sicily and Northern Africa, Sardinia was entitled *Tria Frumentaria Subsidia Rei Publicae* (Three Grain Divisions for the Republic). It was also used as a place of exile. During the reign of Tiberius, in the first century AD, some 4,000 Jews were dispatched to the island, as well as Christians, which incidentally led to the rapid spread of Christianity in Sardinia. Prisoners of exile, slaves and local inhabitants, were put to work on the land, and in mines, where silver, lead and iron were extracted. In short, the islanders were generally abused and it was not until the reign of Augustus that Roman citizenship was granted to a selected few. Augustus also undertook the laying of roads on the island. Four principal arteries were constructed: one along the west coast, which served commercial purposes; another along the east coast which was used for military defense, and two through the interior of the island.

THE MIDDLE AGES

The eventual decline of the Roman Empire, in the fifth century, opened up Sardinia to invaders. In AD455, the Vandals, headed by Genserico, invaded from the shores of North Africa, and held power in Sardinia for 80 years. They were usurped by the Byzantines, whose growing empire, based in present-day Istanbul, claimed Sardinia as one of the seven Byzantine provinces. However, the great distance from Istanbul, the Byzantine seat of rule, meant that their hold on Sardinia was to say the least tenuous, and it was not long before this situation was exploited. In AD711 the Saracens attacked, the first of a series of invasions that were to persist over the next 300 years. Many cities, particularly on the west coast, were destroyed, including *Sulcis, Nora, Teulada* and *Cornus*. There was subsequently a widespread movement of populations from the coastlands to the security of inland regions. The inhabitants of *Turris* (modern Porto Torres) fled inland to Sassari. Populations were also forced to abandon the coasts, due to the worsening scourge of malaria, the inhabitants of the Tirso valley, for example, moving to the mountain town of Nuoro.

It was during this bleak period, with a growing need to defend against the Saracen invaders, that Sardinia entered into an era of judicial rule. In the ninth century, the island was divided into four geographical zones: Calgliari, Arborea, Torres (also known as

Sardinia is not only a land of natural beauty, for there is a variety of historic architecture to be seen

Sardinia is renowned for its clear, blue, seas

The islands greatest asset is its coastline used for both tourism and industry

Logudoro), and Gallura, each of which had its capital in *Calaris* (Cagliari), *Tharros* (Oristano), *Torres* (Porto Torres) and *Civita* (Olbia) respectively. Each zone constituted a judiciary and was headed by a *giudicato* (judge) who was elected from the most important families of the region. The judiciary was sub-divided into *partes* (districts) or *curatorie* (parishes), which roughly corresponded with geographical areas. Villages and small towns were under the auspices of a *maiore* (mayor), while larger towns and cities were controlled by a *curatore* (curator). Borders and seats of power fluctuated, but the general organisation of the island continued in this way for almost five centuries. In the twelfth century, by which time the judiciaries were well-established, Sardinia was divided into 57 *curatorie* (parishes). Twenty of these were in Torres, 13 lay within Arborea, 14 in Cagliari and 10 in Gallura. Society was organised into distinct classes, which had different entitlements, and which people adopted by birthright. The *donnikellos* were the most important families in Sardinia and enjoyed complete freedom. The *liveros* were craftsmen, land-owners and property-owners. The *pauperos* cultivated communal land outside the villages in which they lived. The *servos* or *colivertos*, who made up the majority of the population, were servants and workers.

The first-hand experience of this politico-administrative and economic system, was condensed into the *Carta de Logu*, the first written Code of Laws in Sardinia. It was compiled by the judge, Mariano d'Arborea, and was in use up until the nineteenth century. It was actually published after Mariano's death, by his daughter, Eleonora of Arborea, in 1392. Eleonora of Arborea, often referred to as Sardinia's Joan of Arc, was *giudicata* from 1383 to 1404. Her reign was studded with many heroic deeds, but she is best remembered for her steadfast resistance against the Pisans. Since 1015, when Pisa and Genoa joined forces with Sardinia to fight off the last of the Saracen invaders these two powerful, sea-trading republics had become increasingly involved with the island. In 1205, the judiciary of Gallura ceded control to Pisa. Fifty years later, the Pisans overcame the Genoans in the decisive battle of Santa Igia, and claimed the judiciary of Cagliari. The Genoans looked to the north, where they gained the rather unstable control of the judiciary of Logudoro. The capital of Logudoro, Sassari, did not surrender until 1236, when the Genoan merchant family, the Dorias, arrived, but the Pisans were a continuous threat. The very last judiciary to lose independence was that of Arborea which fell into the control of the Aragonese within a decade of Eleonora's death in 1404.

The period in which the Pisans and Genoans occupied Sardinia gave the island a new lease of life. Agriculture was intensified, new mines were opened, and commerce and industry flourished. Towns were endowed with fine architecture and wealthy Pisan merchants bestowed the land with numerous churches which were built by Tuscan architects to designs modelled on the churches of Pisa, Lucca and Pistoia. However, first Pisa, and then Genoa, fell victim to the rising power of Venice, leaving Sardinia in the hands of the Aragonese.

ARAGONESE CONQUEST AND SPANISH DOMINATION
The Aragonese gained their first foothold in Sardinia in 1297, when Bonifacio VIII gave the exclusive rights of the island to James II, King of Aragon, in return for Sicily. In 1357, the first Aragonese viceroy was installed, and two governments were established, one of which was based in Cagliari and the other in Sassari. It was not until 1478, however, following the Battle of Macomer, that Sardinia was completely subjugated to Aragonese rule. A year later, Aragon and Castile were united with the marriage of Ferdinand and Isabella, and Sardinia was henceforward ruled by unified Spain. The Spanish dominated Sardinia for over 500 years. Their period of rule was consistently grim and led to a drastic fall in the population. At the start of the Aragonese domination, Sardinia had 340,000 inhabitants. In the first Aragonese census of 1483, the population had fallen to 150,000, the lowest in Sardinia's recorded history. The general decline that took hold of Sardinia from the fourteenth through to the sixteenth century was mainly due to the exploitive nature of the Spanish reign. There was a lack of industry, public services and communications, as all public revenue was siphoned off to Spain. The viceroys that controlled the island served 3 year terms and rarely had any real interest in local affairs. While of the 376 *feudi* (fiefs) into which Sardinia was divided, 188 belonged to absent landlords. The Spanish landlords put their property into the charge of a *podatori* (governors), who likewise did not hold Sardinian interests at heart.

The disinterest of Sardinia's rulers, led to an increase in banditry and an outbreak of vendettas. It also left the coasts unguarded, and before long, Sardinia suffered a series of Saracen raids, just as it had done in the Middle Ages. In addition to this, the island suffered its most terrible attacks of malaria, namely in 1404, 1479, 1529 and 1582, with the worst in 1652 and 1655, which took tens of thousands of lives. Conditions did not show any signs of improving until the reign of Philip II who undertook the construction of sixty watch-towers along the coasts, most of which remain standing today. Philip IV continued the good works of his predecessor, improving the administration of the island and founding new agricultural schemes which involved the re-population of Campidano, Capo Terra and *Sulcis*, which had suffered depopulation earlier on in the era. It was during this period too that the universities were opened in Sassari and Cagliari.

THE SAVOY PERIOD

In 1714, during the Spanish War of Succession, Sardinia passed into the control of the Hapsburg dynasty. However, 4 years later the Treaty of London, saw Sardinia given to the House of Savoy in exchange for Sicily. The appointment of Vittorio Amedeo as viceroy of Sardinia in 1720, heralded a new era of optimism. Intensive reforms, which included the elimination of banditry and also the re-organisation of postal services, transformed the island. Some of the most positive reforms took place between 1750 and 1773 under G. Battista Bogino, who was the first governor of Sardinia to fully understand the extent to which the island had been over-exploited. G. Battista Bogino's term ended with the death of King Carlo Emanuele III. However, Amedeo III, who was on the throne from 1773 to 1796, saw that living conditions continued to improve in Sardinia. The rising standards of living were reflected in the increasing population which in 1782 had risen to 436,000. It was also evident in the new towns that appeared, such as Carloforte in 1737, and Calsetta in 1770.

Towards the end of the eighteenth century, attention was turned towards the growing threat of Napoleon, who loitered with his fleets along the shores of Sardinia. However, in 1821, with King Carlo Felice on the throne, further reforms were made, namely in agriculture and education. Radical improvements were made in communications too, as the highway Carlo Felice, the main artery from Cagliari to Porto Torres testifies to this day. King Carlo Alberto succeeded Carlo Felice in 1831 and achieved further progress with the organisation of a postal service to the mainland in 1835, the abolition of feuds in 1836, and the annexation of Sardinia to Piedmont, which meant it adopted Piedmontese law. The population continued to expand, reaching 547,000 in 1848.

ITALIAN UNIFICATION

Carlo Alberto's son, Vittorio Emanuele II, became the first King of unified Italy in 1861, following the victorious campaign of Garibaldi. Two years after his succession to the throne, Sardinia was equipped

Most of Sardinia's rural population look to sheep farming as a form of income

The Sardinian landscape is scattered with evidence of Nuraghic settlements

with a railway system and the 'Sardinia Question' sought the answer to the island's perennial problems concerning agriculture, roads, hygiene and illiteracy. Under the Fascist government of Mussolini, many of these problems were addressed with schemes to improve agriculture and social conditions. Vast areas of marshes were reclaimed and irrigated, and new towns were built. The population burgeoned, leaping from 859,000 in 1921 to 1,004,000 in 1936.

World War II left Sardinia badly damaged, particularly the capital, Cagliari. However, public works were soon resumed and in 1948, Sardinia was made an autonomous region of Italy. In the same year, the US Rockefeller Foundation eradicated the malaria that still afflicted the coastal regions. By 1951 the population was 1,269,000. Today, Sardinia has a population of over 1 ½ million. The most recent boom to its economy has been tourism which has snowballed ever since the Emerald Coast was made one of the top European holiday destinations by Agha Khan in the 1960s. Like Southern Italy, the island is less wealthy than the northern regions of the mainland, although cities, such as Sassari, enjoy an increasingly high standard of living. The island was supported by the Cassa per il Mezzogiorno, a scheme that was introduced in the 1950s to develop the poorer South. The development of service industries has overtaken agriculture, and traditional ways of life have largely given way to a consumer society. However, Sardinia retains its character, which has partly been shaped by its long history of exploitation and abuse, and the visitor will find much of unique charm beneath the veneer of twentieth-century progress.

GEOGRAPHY

The island of Sardinia is situated almost in the centre of the West Mediterranean basin, to the west of the Italian peninsula, although mainland Italy and North Africa are virtually equidistant, being approximately 180km (112 miles) away, measured at their closest points. The French island of Corsica lies just 12km (7 miles) from the northern tip of Sardinia, the Balearic islands are 315km (195 miles) to the west and the Italian island of Sicily is 278km (172 miles) to the south. In short, it has a key position and has long attracted traders and merchants, particularly since the opening of the Suez Canal, which secured the island a place on the through Mediterranean trade route. The island's many fine, natural harbours, including the ample bays of the Golfo dell'Asinara in the north, the Golfo di Orosei in the east, the Golfo di Cagliari in the south, and the Golfo di Oristano in the west, have also helped to attract passing traffic.

With a coastline of over 1,800km (1,116 miles) long, Sardinia is by no means a small island, for including the offshore islets, it has a total area of 24,089sq km (9,260sq miles), making it the second largest island in the Mediterranean. From Punta del Falcone, which is the northernmost point, to Capo Teulada, the southernmost point, is 270km (167 miles). The width of the island is 96km (60 miles) at its narrowest part and 145km (90 miles) at its widest, and is shaped like an irregular quadrangle, with its shortest sides running south-west and north-east respectively. The shape has been likened to a footprint, or a sandal as in the case of the ancient Greeks, who named the island *Sandaliotis*.

Sardinia, however, has not always been an island. Many eons ago, when the level of the sea was lower, Sardinia was connected to the mainland by a peninsula that jutted out from Tuscany. Unlike the mainland, however, where the Alps and Apennines form the backbone of the peninsula, Sardinia has no mountain chains as such, but rather massifs which are surrounded by plains and plateaux, although none of the massifs are very high. The most impressive is the Gennargentu Massif which rises in the central part of the island. It contains the tallest peak in Sardinia, La Marmora, which has a summit 1,834m (6,015ft) above sea level.

Unlike Corsica, Sardinia lacks the dramatic beauty of mountains. Less than 15 per cent of the island is covered in mountains of over 500m (1,640ft), and the average altitude is 334m (1,095ft), compared to 568m (1,863ft) in Corsica. The landscape is nonetheless hilly and there are many grand outcrops of dramatically-sculpted, granite rock as well as table mountains and *giare* (plateaux) that protrude from the plains like natural fortresses. Plains and plateaux are a common feature of the landscape. The largest plain is the Campidano in the southern part of the island. It forms a huge belt from the Golfo di Oristano to the Golfo di Cagliari which is 110km (68 miles) long and 15km (9 miles) to 25km (15 ½ miles) wide. It is here that most of the island's agriculture is concentrated.

Only a third of the island has arable soils. Granite, schist and volcanic rock cover well over half of the land. Not surprisingly, therefore, most of Sardinia's rural population look to sheep farming as a form of income. There are some 25,000 shepherds roaming the hills, and almost four million sheep, which accounts for a third of the total sheep in Italy. The cultivation of cork trees is another means of income. The cork oak thrives on granite soils and northern Sardinia produces most of the corks used in Italy's massive wine production.

Sardinia also has a prosperous fishing industry, particularly along the west coast where shoals of tuna and mullet pass by in the migratory season. The coast has coral reefs too, the main ones being between Capo Caccia and Capo Testa at a depth of 100m (328ft) to 200m (656ft) deep, although they are now largely depleted. Salt is another product of the coast, especially along the flat southern and western shores where there are some 15,000 hectares (37,050 acres) of lagoons, marshes and bogs. Twelve thousand hectares (29,640 acres) of the wetland areas are designated of international importance for the preservation of wildlife and birds such as flamingoes.

REGIONS

For purposes of administration, Sardinia is divided into four provinces, which roughly correspond with the four judicial regions that existed in the Middle Ages. The largest is the province of Cagliari which has a population of 728,548. Sassari is the second largest, with a population of 431,986. Nuoro and Oristano, third and fourth respectively. The provinces are named after the four provincial capital cities. The other principal cities on the island are Alghero and Olbia.

Each province is sub-divided into *comune* (communes) or *municipio* (municipalities), rather as it was during the Spanish rule of the island. Most of the sub-divisions fall into natural geographical areas, such as the Sarcidano which is typified by its extensive plain. The names of some of these areas, such as the mountainous central region of the Barbagia, have been in use since Roman times. Other names are derived from those that were used for episcopal seats in the Byzantine era, such as the south-western corner of the island which is known as the Iglesiente.

The *Visitors Guide to Sardinia* explores a good number of these historical territories as well as the provincial capitals and main towns and cities. Geographical points of interest, such as weirdly-eroded granite and trachyte rock are also featured, as are places of natural beauty, including the isolated inland areas and little-visited stretches of the coastline.

1

THE NORTH-EAST

Chapter 1 follows Sardinia's eastern coast, from the bay of Olbia, where most visitors arrive, either by air or by ferry, to the beautiful gulf of Orosei, before heading inland towards the mountainous region of the Barbagia which is the starting point of Chapter 2. Most of the journey is made on the SS125 Orientale Sarda, a winding but reasonably surfaced road, which dawdles through low, rocky hills, smothered in *macchia* (Mediterranean scrub), and along the coastline which is a mixture of marshy lagoons, cultivated alluvial plains and majestic limestone cliffs, sheltering sandy bays. There are plenty of opportunities for bathing along the way, and those in search of paradise may well be satisfied by taking a hired boat from one of the resorts to any of the numerous idyllic coves along the coast that are not accesible by road. Most resorts have a good range of accommodation and there are many camping sites, usually pleasantly positioned in pine forests overlooking the sea.

Other attractions on the route include caves, in which stalagmites and stalactites can be seen, and small, rural towns where tourism has brought back to life some of the folk crafts that were on the verge of dying out. Textiles are woven to traditional designs, wood and cork are sculpted and carved, and there is tooled leather, colourful ceramics and metalwork too. The crafts are generally of a high standard and are exported widely throughout Europe.

The route also offers gastronomic delights such as fresh lobster, *arragosta*, which is to be found at most coastal resorts, and excellent *pecorino Sardo*, sheep's cheese, which is made in the inland towns. In the hills backing the gulf of Orosei, visitors will find the winegrowing domain of Cannonau. This is one of the most popular red wines in Sardinia and is typically robust and heady, with sweeter versions having something in common with port.

Route 1A • Olbia to Posada

Olbia is the most important port on the East coast of Sardinia and is ever-busy with the to and fro of traffic from mainland Italy. The port is the closest point on the island to the mainland, and is advantageously positioned in a deep, natural inlet which is enclosed by low, craggy headlands. The town is made up of modern, whitewashed buildings which sprawl across the plain, separated from the port area by a busy main road and railway line.

Despite its modern aspect, the origins of Olbia go back to the fourth-century BC when the Carthaginians established a sea-trading colony here. In 295BC, the Romans, expelling the Carthaginians, made Olbia a foothold from which to invade the rest of Sardinia. They built three main highways, connecting Olbia to the rest of the island, which initially served military value, but later became major trade routes. With the decline of the Roman Empire, Olbia suffered a series of invasions by the Saracens and the Vandals, from the fifth century onwards, and it was not until the twelfth century that the town once more rose to prominence, this time under the control of the wealthy merchants of Pisa. It was completely rebuilt and given the new name of Terranova, by which it was known until 1939, when it reverted to Olbia. Following on from the Pisans, the town became the capital of the local rulers, the Giudicato di Gallura, and continued to prosper up until the sixteenth century, when Olbia was razed to the ground by the Turks, who were allied with the French, against King Charles V.

The remnants of Olbia's colourful past are, not surprisingly, few and far between. The most impressive monument to have survived is the little, twelfth-century church of San Simplicio which stands testimony to the era of Pisan rule. It is placed on a small piazza, near the railway station, in the north-west corner of the town. Built of a sombre, granite stone, it has a façade typical of the Pisan-Romanesque style with a triple-mullioned window in the high, central section, and slender, blind arcades decorating the outer walls. A plain doorway leads into the interior which has an interesting collection of locally-found Roman tombs and inscription stones, displayed along the side aisles. Some of the columns lining the central aisle are also Roman in origin, and the font is made from a Roman funerary urn.

It is also worth strolling along the town's main street, Corso Umberto, which is lined with smart cafés, restaurants and fashionable shops. At the eastern end of Corso Umberto there is a crafts centre run by I.S.O.L.A. (Istituto Sardo Organizzazione Lavoro

Artigianato), a Sardinian organisation for the promotion and marketing of local crafts. The centre has a permanent exhibition of Sardinian crafts, ranging from objects made of cork and wood, to pottery, textiles and basket work.

Leave Olbia by the fly-over spanning the port, and follow signs to Nuoro on the SS125. The road follows the coast southwards, past the imposing off-shore island, **Tavolara**. This grand, prism-shaped island is over 70 million years old, having been formed in the Mesozoic era. A few people inhabit its gently sloping western end, but the other parts of the island are steep and inaccessible, with its dramatic, limestone cliffs plunging straight down into the sea. The cliffs culminate in a high plateau which is 565m (1,853ft) above sea level at its highest point. Those who wish to visit the island should stop at the small resort of **Porto San Paolo**, 14km (9 miles) south-east of Olbia, from where hourly tours depart from the Pontile della Marina. There is good underwater swimming to be had around the rocky periphery of the island, and the numerous small coves and inlets make for an interesting exploration by boat.

The SS125 continues south along the coastline, which is predominantly rocky, and covered with *macchia* (Mediterranean scrub) and small cork trees which find a way up between the boulders. Occasionally the jagged rocks give way to a sandy bay where there is the inevitable cluster of holiday villas or resort hotels, all of which enjoy fine views of the Tavolara island. To the south of the Tavolara, is another flat-topped island, **Isola Molara**, which is by comparison quite small, standing little over 150m (492ft) above sea level. The island is barren and uninhabited and is best admired from the jagged promontory of **Capo Coda Cavallo** (Horse Tail Cape), which is less than 3km (2 miles) offshore.

From Capo Coda Cavallo, the route proceeds southwards alongside the expansive, marshy lagoon, **Stagno di San Teodoro**, which is a haven for wildlife and birds, including flamingoes in the migratory season. **San Teodoro**, 8km (5 miles) south of Capo Coda Cavallo, is one of the better-established resorts along this rapidly-developing stretch of the coast. Positioned just inland from the sea, the resort brims with accommodation and restaurants, all of which are very busy in August. There are two excellent beaches within a kilometre (½ mile) of San Teodoro. The first is **La Cinta** (The Belt) which is a fine, sand spit, to the north of the resort. The spit encloses the mouth of the lagoon and the water is shallow and safe for bathing. The second beach is at **Cala d'Ambra**, a vast, sandy bay which lies at the other side of a small hill, to the south of San Teodoro. It is less sheltered than La Cinta, but is magnificently situated with small

 rocks scattered offshore, and fine views of the Tavolara and Molara islands.

The route continues south of San Teodoro along the SS125. A new road has been constructed here, but the old road offers the more picturesque scenery, passing through the undulating, *macchia*-covered hills before rejoining the coast at **Budoni**. There are several good sandy beaches south of Budoni which are backed by attractive forests of umbrella pines. The most easily accessible of these are **Porto Ainu**, 4km (2 ½ miles) south of Budoni, which surrounds a charming bay, and **Pineta al Mare**, a further 7km (4 miles) south. The latter is reached by a track through the pine forests, which is signposted on the left just before crossing the Posada river. The Posada river forms a wide estuary, in the midst of which, the village of **Posada** clings to the shoulder of a protruding, limestone crag. At the summit of the crag is the ruined fortress, the Castello della Fava. Built by the local *giudice* of Gallura in the twelfth century, it successfully withstood a series of Moorish invasions, although it fell to the Aragonese in the fourteenth century. The history of the castle is steeped in legend and romance, as is the origin of its rather unusual name, which means 'bean'. The story goes, that the Galluran *giudice* were on the point of surrender to the Moors, when they had the idea of sending out a homing pigeon with a message to a fictitious army for reinforcements. The pigeon was sent out with a broadbean in its gullet and the message tied to its foot. According to plan, the bird was shot down by the Moors, who, on finding the bean, deduced that the castle still had a plentiful supply of food, and that Galluran reinforcements were at hand. The Moors thus beat a hasty retreat.

To visit Posada, turn left off the SS125 and follow the narrow road which winds up from the estuary to the village edge. A few parking spaces are to be found on Via Eleonora D'Arborea, just inside the village gate, alternatively park below the walls. On foot, follow Via Eleonora D'Arborea, past the small hotel at the centre of the village, and take the footpath, Via Castello, on the left. The path climbs steeply up to the crenellated fortress walls, inside of which is the tall, square tower of the keep. A wooden staircase leads up to the third floor of the keep from where a metal ladder gives access to the parapet at the top. The views from here are excellent, taking in the wide estuary which is filled with neat citrus groves and banks of bamboo, and the coast, where reedy lagoons and marshes meet the water's edge.

Route 1B • Posada to Orosei

From Posada, visitors may wish to continue along the coast to the expanding resort of **La Caletta**, where there are several kilometres of gently sloping, sandy beaches that are ideally suited for children. The route however, heads inland, on the SS125, for 7 ½km (4 ½ miles) to **Siniscola**, which was once the capital of the Posada Barony. The town lies at the foot of Monte Albo, a dramatic range of bare, rocky mountains that rise abruptly from the flat estuary bed of the Siniscola river. The range is extraordinarily sheer, and culminates in contorted and rugged peaks, well over 1,000m (3,280ft) high. The severe austerity of these mountains is part of the town's character, which, according to D. H. Lawrence, has always lacked charm: 'It is just a narrow, crude, stony place, hot in the sun, cold in the shade.'

However, although Siniscola does not offer historic monuments or picturesque streets, over the last decade it has become a highly productive centre of crafts. The crafts, which include pottery and textiles, are done for commercial purposes, but many of the skills still used, have been handed down over generations. Local costume has also survived to some extent. Many of the elder women wear the traditional, black mourning dress and a long, black apron and black headscarf. The more elaborate costumes, however, for which Siniscola is known throughout Sardinia, are worn only at traditional marriage ceremonies and other special events.

The other attraction of Siniscola is its proximity to the Monte Albo mountains. A scenic drive can be made by continuing along the main road to Nuoro, which follows along the base of the Monte Albo range. Alternatively, a long hike can be made along the mountain tops, by following the trail from Cantoniera di Sant'Anna to Lula. Those intending to undertake this hike should carry plenty of drinking water as there are no supplies along the way. **Lula**, which marks the south-western end of Monte Albo, is well-known for its festival celebrating the Feast of San Francesco di Lula, during which, traditional costumes, similar to those of Siniscola, are worn.

From Siniscola follow the river back to the coast where the small resort of **Santa Lucia** sits proudly on a headland with its robust, circular watch-tower. The resort is at one end of a long, sandy beach which is backed by a dense forest of pine. The road runs alongside the pines, in the shade of which are numerous campsites and holiday villages, to the beautiful bay of **Salina Manna**. The bay is enclosed at the southern end by **Capo Comino**, a dramatic cape with a mass of rocky peaks, whipped up like egg whites, and covered with broom and *macchia*. There is a small village at the tip of the headland, looking across the harbour to the offshore islet, **Isola Ruia**. From the village, there is a panoramic walk along the sand dunes to the south.

It is a 6km (4 miles) hike which can be covered in about 2 hours. The trail is also popular for horse-riding excursions.

The road continues inland from the shore, south of Capo Comino, through the wild and uninhabited Baronia hills. The road undulates through a harsh, rocky landscape, carpeted with the pungentlyscented *macchia*, and then gradually heads down to a majestic pine forest which sweeps down to the sea. A fine, sandy beach extends along the edge of the forest, and can be reached by following the track, signposted to **Cala Ginepro**, which is on the left, just after crossing the river Sos Alinos. The next turning on the left, which follows alongside the river, leads to the resort of **Cala Liberotto**, where there is another beach, as well as a wide range of hotels and restaurants, clustered around the small harbour at the river mouth.

The route proceeds southwards through the lonely Baronia hills, on the SS125, which gradually climbs up onto a desolate, boulder-strewn tableland, from where there are excellent views. The sea crashes on dark rocks far below, while ahead is the magnificent Gulf of Orosei, ringed by the white limestone cliffs that are thought to be the last place of refuge of the Monk Seal. From the other side of the tableland, the road descends to the Cedrino river which winds a lazy course, between tall clumps of bamboo and reed, to the sea. The wide estuary formed around the Cedrino, formerly a malarial swamp, is now neatly planted with almond orchards, citrus groves and market gardens. Seated on the banks of the river is the historic town of Orosei, which is reached by forking right after the bridge.

Known as *Fanum Orisi* in Roman times, Orosei was once a sea-faring town with an important harbour. Its history is punctuated with raids by pirates, Turks and Moors, who attacked from the sea. However, over the centuries, the Cedrino river has gradually silted up and Orosei is now some 3km (2 miles) inland. Many of its inhabitants have moved, with the shoreline, to the new resort built at the mouth of the river. **Marina di Orosei**, which has a popular beach. Orosei has been left with a romantic abandoned air, its once grand buildings crumbling and decaying.

The time of **Orosei's** heyday was during the period of Aragonese power when a series of awesome barons occupied the local seat of rule. Amongst the most imposing figures of this era was Salvatore Guiso who expanded his barony to include both Galtello and Orosei. The character of the town is still Spanish-influenced, an observation that D.H. Lawrence made when he passed through. He wrote of Orosei that it had '… a strange Spanish look, neglected, arid, yet with a bigness and a dilapidated dignity…'

That was how Lawrence described the town's central square, Piazza Popolo, which is presided over by the grand, Baroque façade, of San Giacomo Maggiore. The façade, with its great, white-painted pilasters, was added during the seventeenth century when the original thirteenth-century church was greatly modified and en-larged. The cluster of terracotta tiled roofs date from this earlier

San Giacomo Maggiore church, Orosei

period as do the side walls of the church which are constructed of a sombre, dark stone. To admire the outer walls and the pretty roofs take the steps up, to the left of San Giacomo Maggiore, to Piazza G. Asproni. This small piazza also holds the remains of the town fort, which at one time doubled as the local jail, hence its name, Castello Prigione Vecchia. It was built in the fourteenth century.

Back on Piazza Popolo, there are many attractive narrow streets to explore leading off from the square, and an *itinerario storico*, historic itinerary, is clearly signposted around the main areas of interest. The itinerary starts from the right side of San Giacomo Maggiore and heads downhill past a grand dilapidated mansion, the Casa Rettorale, to the town's lower piazza where there is the ruined novice's quarters of Sant'Antonio del Fuoco, which dates from the fifteenth century. There are many fine examples of Spanish architecture dotted about the town's old quarter, and other churches worth looking out for include, San Gavino and the remains of San Sebastiano.

Route 1C • Orosei to Dorgali

Route 1c leave Orosei by following signs to Dorgali on the SS125. The road climbs up from the Cedrino river estuary, into the foothills of the great Gennargentu mountains. Olive groves and almond orchards cover the lower slopes, while higher up there are extensive marble and granite quarries. Before long, the road climbs sufficiently for there to be fine views of the coast and also of the Cedrino river estuary. Straight ahead the rugged peaks of the Gennargentu gradually loom larger and the landscape becomes very dry and rocky. It is in this inhospitable terrain, that the Cannonau grape thrives, and after 14km (9 miles) from Orosei, the visitor enters the official **Cannonau** wine-making zone. Cannonau is the most widely-grown variety of dark grape in Sardinia, and is used in the production of both dry and sweet red wines. The grape is said to have been introduced by the Spanish and is the equivalent of the French Grenache. The wine is amongst the most popular reds to be drunk by Sardinians and is usually of good quality.

Just after entering the Cannonau wine region, there is a turning on the left to the impressive cavern, **Grotta di Ispinigoli**, or the **Abisso delle Vergini** as it is also called, after the sacrifice of young girls that took place here in ancient times. The road to the cavern skirts around the mountain into which the cave is hollowed, and after 2km (1 mile) forks right and winds around a steep hairpin bend to a large carpark where there is a hotel and restaurant. The cavern entrance, which is at an altitude of 400m (1,312ft), is a further 20m (22yd) up a flight of steps, to the right of the hotel. Inside, one finds oneself at the edge of a vast abyss which drops abruptly to a depth of 80m (262ft). At the centre of this abyss, there stands a monumental stalagmite, 38m (125ft) tall, the second largest in the world after that in Florida which is 2m (7ft) taller. It was at the foot of this megalith that small human bones were discovered, hence leading to the cavern's popular name. It has been difficult to prove that they were the bones of girls, least of all virgins, however, sacrifice undoubtedly did take place here, probably during the Phoenician period, as other sacrificial offerings and pieces of jewellery, dating from this era, were discovered alongside the bones, all which are now on display in the museum in Nuoro. The cavern is well-illuminated, showing the stalagtites and calcarious formations to good effect. The guided tour involves descending the staircase to the abyss floor.

The route continues on the SS125 through a neatly tended landscape where vineyards and olive groves are divided by attractive walls made with the stones collected from the fields. After 7km (4 miles) the road starts to climb the rocky slopes of Monte Bardia, at the foot of which lies the town of **Dorgali**. It is a relatively new town, the medieval settlement being destroyed in an earthquake, and its appearance is rather disshevelled and grim. However, it is a thriving centre of Sardinian crafts and an excellent place to buy local produce, as well as being a good base from which to explore the nearby Gulf of Orosei with its caves and spectacular beaches.

The town sprawls lengthwise along a snaking high street which is lined with ateliers, often called *laboratorio*, and artisan shops. In the *laboratorio*, women can be seen working at vertical looms, that have changed very little in design over the last millennium, knotting carpets in thickly-spun wool which comes from the local sheep. They weave a variety of designs, sometimes copies from twentieth-century artists, such as Miro, and at other times using the more traditional motifs, which include stylised animals such as peacocks and horses. The colours of the traditional carpets are generally limited to a cream ground with the design areas woven in black and red. Other crafts available in Dorgali include leather work, jewellery, ceramics and objects made from cork and wood. The wooden masks that are quite commonly seen are reproductions of those worn at the Mamuttones festival. Mamuttones, or Mamutti, is the local dialect for the devil, and during the festival, which takes place on Shrove Tuesday, the masked Mamutti parade around wearing sheepskin hides and carrying great bundles of bells on their backs. For local produce go to any food shop, but the wine is probably best bought direct from a *cantina* (wine shop), a number of which are dotted about the town's outskirts. The Rosso di Dorgali is well worth trying as although it is not classified as a DOC, it is one of Sardinia's most reputable Cannonau wines. A good selection of both wine and food can be found in the Prodotti Alimentari Sardi, a well-stocked shop on the *strada panoramica* which runs parallel with the main street, above the top of the town. It is reached by following the SS125 in the direction of Cala Gonone and taking the first left.

To get to the coastal resort of **Cala Gonone**, which is a total 7km (4 miles) from Dorgali, follow the SS125 out of the town and take the second turning on the left. The road proceeds downwards, through a tunnel which ends in a large bend, to be approached with caution. The road emerges at the other side of the mountains, high above the spectacular Gulf of Orosei. It was over this pass, which cuts between Monte Bardia (882m/2,893ft) and Monte Tului (915m/3,001ft), now a popular spot for hang-gliding, that the Carthaginians retreated from the invading Romans. The Carthaginians had settled at Cala Gonone on the site of a Phoenician colony. However, the growing power of the Roman Empire forced them back into the mountains where they established the original settlement of Dorgali. Traces of the ancient site have been uncovered just outside the modern-day resort, the remains, however, are scant.

As the road hairpins down to the resort there are several parking lay-bys from which to admire the magnificent views across the gulf which has 40km (25 miles) of virtually unspoilt coastline. Cala Gonone itself is the only major development. It is situated at the centre of the gulf and is amongst the most popular beach resorts on the island. Its popularity is due to the stunning scenery, excellent beaches and the wealth of caves and grottoes to explore.

Excursions along the bay are best made by hiring a boat from the resort. Amongst the most popular excursion is to the **Grotta del Bue Marino** (Grotto of Sea Oxen) which lies 2km (1 mile) south of Cala Gonone. Until 10 years ago, the cave was inhabited by the monk seal (also known as sea-oxen), and although it is thought that the seal still inhabits other parts of the Gulf of Orosei, only four sightings have been made in recent times. The species requires vast feeding grounds and sheltered places for reproduction, so that the only hope of saving the monk seal from extinction is to keep long stretches of the coast free of human habitations.

Grotta del Bue Marino is of karst origin and has a wide, gaping mouth with a central pillar which has been eroded over the centuries by wave action. Boats chug into the mouth of the cave and visitors disembark at a small pier, from where the tour is continued on foot.

The Cannonau grape is the most widely grown variety of dark grape in Sardinia

Dorgali is a thriving centre of Sardinian crafts

There are two main arms which extend for some 5km (3 miles), only 1km (½ mile) of which is illuminated and accessible to the visitor. The highlights of the tour are the bizarre formations that have formed over the centuries, some of which have been attributed to popular features, such as Dante's profile (*profilo di Dante*), the pie (*la torta*) and the hall of organs (*sala dell'organo*).

Boats can also be taken to other caves along the bay, as well as to beaches such as **Cartoee** and **Osalla** which are to the north of Cala Gonone, and to **Cala Luna** (Moon Beach) and **Cala Sisine**, which are both to the south. The beaches found along the bay lie mostly in the lee of dramatic limestone cliffs where myrtle, oleander and hardy shrubs sprout in profusion. The cliffs are the domain of large colonies of the Eleonora Falcon which nest here between June and October.

Those keen on hiking may be interested in the 4-day trail which heads south from Cala Gonone to **Baunei**. The trail is mostly inland from the coast and a good map, food and a tent are essential. The Istitutu Geografico Militare produce the best large scale maps, but they are generally hard to come by and should be ordered from a map specialist before setting out. It is also possible to explore the gulf by canoe. Three day expeditions are organised which cover about 40km (24 miles), from Cala Gonone to Santa Maria Navarrese.

Those who prefer to explore the Gulf of Orosei by road, can head south of Dorgali on the SS125. The road winds inland from the shore, high along the mountain tops, from where there are exceptional views of the coast. The mountains are wild and uninhabited and the road twists toruously from one pass to the next, the highest being that of Genna Silana, which is 1,050m (3,444ft) above sea level. Baunei, which marks the southern end of the Gulf of Orosei is 50km (31 miles) south of Dorgali. It is a popular centre for hiking, although the surrounding mountains are steep and quite challenging.

Route 1D • Dorgali to Oliena

From Dorgali, return back along the SS125 in the direction of Orosei. After 3km (2 miles), turn left and follow the SS129 which heads gently down to the Cedrino river, one of the three principal waterways in Sardinia. A concrete viaduct, 199m (653ft) high, spans the Cedrino, which is joined at this point by another large, but usually dry river, the Fiumineddu. Hikers may be interested in the 5-hour trail that follows the Fiumineddu river, southwards to the impressive canyon of Gola su Gorruppu which is some 500m (1,640ft) deep. The path is reasonably well-marked, but a map, such as that published by the Istituto Geografico Militario of the Monte Oddeu, is needed. To cross over the gorge, adequate climbing equipment is also necessary.

Shortly after crossing the viaduct turn right, following signs for the SS129 and SS131. The road winds gently up between groves of olives and dry-stone walls. After 1km (½ mile) the ancient site of **Nuraghe Noriolo** is passed on the right. The site is unexcavated and the only evidence of its existence are the vague mounds in the earth, standing amongst the olive trees. However, a further 2km (1 mile) north, there is another Nuraghic site which has far more evidence and is well-preserved. **Serra Orrios**, as it is called, is romantically placed in the midst of the countryside with gnarled olive trees and prickly pear cactii growing all around. To reach the site, park next to the gates on the right side of the road from where there is a signpost to *Villagio Nuragico*. Proceed on foot along the track, heading towards a group of farm buildings. Before reaching the farm buildings, an antiquated steam roller is passed on the right, from where arrows point the way to the Nuraghe Oveni. This is a Nuraghic fortification, sited in the north corner of the field, rather overgrown by the rampant prickly pear cactii. The structure is of an irregular shape, and is built with hefty blocks of grey stone, in much the same style as the dry-stone walls that surround the fields, and is defended by two sections of curved walls. Access is at the back, up a rough series of rock steps.

Return across the field to the steam roller and follow the red arrows, which are painted on the rocks at regular intervals, to the left side of the farm buildings. It is a pleasant walk from here, of about 600m (656yd), along an old, partially-cobbled lane, which passes between olive groves. The entrance to the site is through a gate on the left. The settlement is comprised of about seventy habitations, most of which are circular. There is a well-preserved example immediately on the right after passing through the gate. On the left, there are the foundations of what is believed to be a sacred precinct. Two large slabs of stone mark the entrance way and the eastern end is curved like an apse with a passage running behind it. Beyond the sacred precinct, a maze of footpaths weave in and out of the neat, circular houses which are overgrown with shrubs and olive trees. At the northern side of the site there is a large temple precinct. Stone paving slabs cover the floor of a large central room which has a series of small chambers leading off either side, while a channel runs through the centre of the building, possibly for draining rain water. The finds that were discovered at the site during the excavation in 1938, include ceramics, bronzes and objects of stone, and are now on display in the Cagliari Archaeological Museum.

From Serra Orrios, return to the Cedrino river valley and turn right, following the road in the direction of Oliena. The road proceeds along a wide basin where the Cannonau grape grows in profusion, while to the left, there rises the dramatic limestone wall of the Sopramonte plateau. This impressive limestone mass is bounded by the mountains of Oliena, Orgosolo, Dorgali and Urzulei and culminates in the peak of Monte Corrasi which is 1,463m (4,799ft) high. It is totally wild and uninhabited, and was a popular hideout in times past for bandits, being riddled with gullies, ravines and caves. Now it is a projected area for development as a National Park where it is planned to protect the griffon-vulture, which is on the point of extinction, the golden eagle and the moufflon, a type of wild mountain sheep found only in Sardinia and Corsica. It is also planned to preserve the dense forests of holm-oak which grow in the interior and have never been cut, a phenomenon quite rare to Italy. Another feature of the Sopramonte are the *pinetta*, small, conical huts built of stones and branches since time immemorial to shelter shepherds.

After 8km (5 miles) from the Serra Orrios junction, an excursion to the edge of the Sopramonte can be made by turning left to **Su Gologone**. The road ends after 2km (1 mile) at a holiday centre, where there is a hotel, and a restaurant which is well-reputed for its traditional Sardinian cuisine. There are also two tennis courts, an 18-hole mini-golf course, two bowling greens, a horse-riding centre and a swimming pool which is filled with the fresh mountain water from the nearby source. The source gushes from high in a cleft in the limestone rock above the Fratale river bed. Nearby is the charming little white church, Nostra Signora della Pieta and the tumbled down remains of San Giovanni. Those planning to spend time here may wish to join one of the excursions organised at the holiday centre. The excursion up the Lanaittu valley is particularly recommended and includes a hike up the slopes of the Sopramonte to the remains of the Nuraghic village of *Tiscali*. Also in the Lanaittu valley, are numerous karsitic caves, amongst the most complex of which are Sa Oche and Su Bentu which are linked by an underground system of channels, covering some 12km (7 miles). The grotto of Corbeddu, named after a group of bandits, is included on the same itinerary and has yielded evidence of ancient civilisations.

The route continues along the Oliena river bed, past the church of Monserrata on the left, after which there are views across the valley, on the right, to Nuoro. The road then gradually climbs up to the little mountain town of Oliena, which is the starting point of Route 2a in Chapter 2.

A prickly pear cactus

The Nuraghic site of Serra Orrios

Additional Information

Places to Visit

Cala Gonone
Grotta del Bue Marino
Guided tours by boat from Cala Gonone daily 9am, 10am, 11am, 3pm, 1 April-15 October. Winter 3pm (minimum 20 people) organise privately with boat company: Uffici Trasporti Marittimi, Cala Gonone
☎ 0784 93305

Dorgali
Grotta di Ispinigoli
7km (4 miles) north-east Dorgali
☎ (0784) 96243
Open: April to October, obligatory guided tour (lasts 45min). 9, 10 and 11am, 12noon, 1, 3, 4 and 5pm (in July, August and September additional tour at 6pm). October to March, only open by advanced booking at Pro Loco in Dorgali for groups of 20 or over.

Laboratorio Artigiano (Textile Centre)
Caterina Spanu Mesina
Via La Marmora 32
☎ (0784) 96163

Olbia
I.S.O.L.A
Istituto Sardo Organizzazione Lavoro Artigianato
Sardinian Institute for Associations of Craft Work
Corso Umberto 28
☎ 0789 26525
Open: daily 9am-12noon, 3-6pm.

Su Gologone
Centro Vacanze Su Gologone
Residenza Turistica
☎ 0784 287512 or 287552
Open: March to October.

Useful Information

Cala Gonone
Events and Festivals
Cala Gonone
Last Saturday May, Sagra del Pesce. (Fish Festival, fresh fish is fried at the quayside and sold along with local wine and wafer-thin *carasu* bread. There is also a market of local produce, wines, cheeses, sweets and crafts from Dorgali. The festival ends with a folk dancing display).

Transport
Consorzio Trasporti Marittimi (Ferry)
☎ 0784 93305 or 93302

Dorgali
Tourist Information Centres
Pro Loco
Via Lamarmora
☎ 0784 96243

Comune di Dorgali
☎ 0784 96113

Travel Agencies
Falctour
Via Lamarmora 163
☎ 0784 95170

Emergencies
Carabinieri (Military Police)
☎ 0784 96114

Guardia Medica (Medical Officer)
Via Umberto
☎ 0784 96521

Olbia
Events and Festivals
3rd Sunday May, Festa di San Simplicio. (Festival of patron saint, San Simplicio, who was martyred

in the fourth century. The festival lasts 6 days and includes religious processions, folk dancing displays, poetry recitations, games and fireworks).

24 June, Festa di Sant'Agostino. (St Agostino's Day, 3-day festival).

1st Sunday September, Festa di Santa Lucia. (St Lucia's Day, 3-day festival).

Estate Olbiese (Summer Festival).

Tourist Information Centre
Azienda Autonoma di Soggiorno e
   Turismo
Via Catello Piro 1
☎ 0789 21453

Transport
Aeroporto Costa Smeraldo
   (Airport)
4km (2 miles) SE Olbia
☎ 0789 69400 or 23721
(Hourly shuttle bus from airport to Olbia centre).

Autonoleggio Italia (Car Hire)
Aeroporto Costa Smeralda
☎ 0789 69501

Hertz Italia (Car Hire)
Aeroporto Costa Smeralda
☎ 0789 69389 &
Via Regina Elena 34
☎ 0789 21274

Nolauto (Car Hire)
Aeroporto Costa Smeralda
☎ 0789 69548

Smeralda Express (Car and Vespa
   Hire)
Via Catello Piro 9 ☎ 0789 25512

Ferrovie dello Stato (Railway)
☎ 0789 22477

Tirrenia Navigazione (Ferry)
Corso Umberto 17
☎ 0789 22688

Sardinia Ferries (Ferry)
Corso Umberto 4
☎ 0789 25200

NAV.AR.MA (Ferry)
Corso Umberto 187
☎ 0789 27927

Travel Agencies
Agenzie Marittime Sarde
Via Regina Elena 38
☎ 0789 24137

Alisarda
Corso Umberto 195/c
☎ 0789 69400

Avitur
Corso Umberto 139
☎ 0789 21217

Intours
Corso Umberto 168
☎ 0789 26069

Unimare
Via Principe Umberto 3
☎ 0789 23572

Emergencies
Carabinieri (Military Police)
Via G. d'Annunzio
☎ 0789 21221

Guardia Medica (Medical Officer)
☎ 0789 22394

Ospedale Civile (Hospital)
Viale A. Moro ☎ 0789 58595

Pronto Soccorso (First Aid Service)
☎ 0789 22707

Automobile Club d'Italia
Via Catello Piro 9
☎ 0789 21414

Orosei
Events and Festivals
16-17 January, Festa di Sant'Antonio. (Feast of St Anthony, greasy pole competition).

3rd Sunday May, Festa del Mare. (Festival of the Sea).

23-25 July, Festa di San Giacomo Apostolo. (Religious festival, folk dancing displays, poetry competition and an exhibition of local produce).

Tourist Information Centre
c/o Municipio
Via Nazionale
☎ 0784 98714

Emergencies
Carabinieri (Military Police)
☎ 0784 98722

USL Servizi Sanitari (Medical Care)
Piazza Cavallotti
☎ 0784 98302 or 98303

San Teodoro
Tourist Information Centre
Pro Loco
Via Tirreno 3
☎ 0784 865767

Siniscola
Events and Festivals
2nd Sunday May, San Francesco di Lula. (Procession to the sanctuary of San Francesco in the Albo mountains. The festival, known as the Novenaria, traditionally lasts nine days, during which time pilgrims stay at the sanctuary).

Tourist Information Centre
Comune di Siniscola
☎ 0784 878524

Su Gologone
Emergencies
Carabinieri (Military Police)
☎ 0784 288720

2

BARBAGIA

Chapter 2 travels through the wild, inland region of Barbagia which lies within the modern-day province of Nuoro. The province, which covers over 7,000sq km (2,700sq miles), is mostly mountainous, encompassing some of the highest peaks in Sardinia, but is only accessible along narrow, at times tortuous, roads. The population, apart from in and around the provincial capital of Nuoro, is spread very sparsely, and only shepherds inhabit the *solitudini*, the more remote and lonely areas. Shepherding has long been the main form of livelihood in the region, and over half of Sardinia's four million sheep are reared here. Pastoral life has kept apace with the twentieth century; most shepherds nowadays herd their flocks by van or jeep, and come home at night to comfortable modern homes. Despite this, rural Barbagia remains very much in touch with its long history and ancient traditions.

The history of Barbagia goes back to the days of the Nuraghic settlements that were established in 1800BC, but was given its name in the second-century BC, by the invading Romans who found the mountains defended by 'Barbaricini', a term they applied to anyone who did not belong to the Roman or ancient Greek civilisations. The Barbaricini fought from their Nuraghic strongholds and were well-armed with swords, arrows and lances, which were expertly forged from bronze. The Romans, however, were persistent and the 'Barbaricini' were forced gradually to retreat to higher, and more remote parts of the mountains, although they were never completely conquered. In the centuries to follow, the mountainous interior, which became known as Barbagia, maintained an independent identity and only became fully integrated with the rest of Sardinia following the defeat of the Saracens in the eleventh century.

For the visitor, Barbagia holds many exciting features, ranging from the Nuraghic settlements that pockmark the landscape and the fine collections of Nuraghic weapons and artefacts in the region's museums, to the rustic life and traditional customs of remote mountain villages. Perhaps the most thrilling aspect of Barbagia is, however, the scenery. There are limestone gorges in the Sopramonte mountains and to the south there are the desolate canyons and barren peaks of the Gennargentu, Sardinia's highest mountain range. Summits in the Gennargentu are around 1,800m (5,904ft) in altitude, and in the remotest reaches there are said to be a few surviving species of the moufflon (*Ovis Musimon*). Other wildlife includes birds of prey and wild boar, although the animal by far the most widely seen are sheep, their bells resounding everywhere you go. Forests of holm and acorn oak, chestnut and hazelnut grow up to an altitude of 1,200m (3,800ft) and *macchia* sprouts from every rocky crevice along with broom, arbutus, oleaster and tamarisk.

It is an ideal spot for those keen on hiking, as the mountains climb steadily rather than sharply, allowing even the amateur to go on long distant hikes. The hiking period is generally rather short, with snow lying underfoot at least until May. But the high altitudes and cool temperatures make the region one of the few places on the island where it is comfortable to hike throughout the hot summer months. Those wishing to hike in the Foreste Demaniali (State Forests) need to apply for a pass and authorisation beforehand (see Additional Information at the end of this chapter). It is also useful for hikers to know that during the summer there is always a drought and springs and wells that would normally provide drinking water are likely to be dried up, therefore always carry a plentiful drinking supply.

Being a land of shepherds, the Barbagia offers the visitor excellent sheep's cheeses, including *ricotta* and *pecorino*, and a variety of local dishes made with lamb. *Agnello con Finoccietti* is worth looking out for, a lamb stew with onion, tomato and fennel. Sheep also provide wool for locally woven textiles, including carpets and cloth. A wide range of crafts are produced in Barbagia, but as in the rest of Sardinia these are manufactured for tourists. The provincial capital of Nuoro, takes a more serious approach to crafts and has a research centre as well as an excellent museum documenting the history of folk art.

The route is divided into three stages. Route 2a starts at Oliena which lies at the foot of the great limestone massif, Sopramonte, within a short distance of Nuoro. Route 2b continues into the heart of the Barbagia region to Fonni which lies at the northern edge of the Gennargentu mountains. Route 2c takes the visitor to the southernmost edge of the mountainous interior, from where Route 3 continues south across the Campidano plain.

Route 2A • Oliena and Nuoro

Oliena lies at an altitude of 379m (1,243ft), at the foot of Monte
Corrasi, which is the highest point of the Sopramonte mountain
range. It is a typical Barbagia mountain town, being rather dour and
grey, its houses sprawled along a high street, with no central piazza
or focal point. It is however, notable for its numerous churches, many
of which have attractive bell-towers. The two churches at the town
entrance, Santa Maria and Santa Croce, both date from the fifteenth
century. The parish church, the Parrochiale di Sant'Ignazio, which
stands nearby, was finished in 1660. It is worth going inside this
church to see the fine polyptych of *St Christopher*, by the Sardinian
school, and also a Spanish statue which is carved from wood.

Tradition in Oliena, especially that of jewellery-making, has not
died out. The town has a centuries-old reputation for its goldsmiths
who still make delicate filigree jewellery, set with semi-precious
stones. The town's main livelihood, however, derives from the
production of olive oil, a tradition that goes back for as long as
anyone can remember, and which also gives Oliena its name. The
wearing of traditional costume is something that is dying out, but
you may be lucky enough to see one of the elderly women wearing
their traditional black, woollen shawl which is embroidered with
golden thread and edged with long, silken fringes. The shawls are
also sold in souvenir shops.

Many of the visitors to Oliena are hikers, as the town is a popular
base from which to make the ascent of Monte Corrasi (1,463m/
4,799ft). Club Alpino Italiano, based in Cagliari (see Additional
Information at the end of this chapter), organise climbs from here.
The Pro Loco office in the town may also assist in providing information about footpaths and guides, as will the Cooperativa Enis.
Alternatively, join one of the organised groups from the holiday
centre at Su Gologone. The hike involves a steep climb up to the
limestone plateau (1,200m/3,936ft) of Pradu, from where a path
continues to the natural spring of Daddana.

For those who are interested, Oliena is also conveniently positioned for an excursion to the capital of the province, **Nuoro**. It lies
just under 12km (7 miles) north-west of Oliena, at the foot of Monte
Ortobene. It is reached by following the SP46 in a northerly direction,
crossing a broad rolling valley, which is filled with Cannonau
vineyards and groves of olives. After 7km (4 miles) the SP58 is joined
and the road starts to hairpin up the rugged slopes of Monte
Ortobene to the town outskirts.

This large, sprawling town, was, until the nineteenth century,

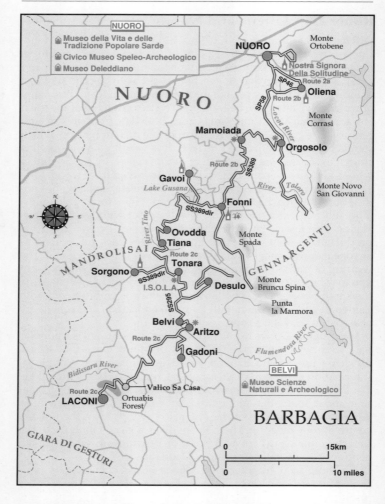

comprised of two villages: Santu Preddu on the upper slopes, and Seuna below. The two villages had a total population of under 3,000. Today, Nuoro is rapidly expanding and fairly industrial, with a population of around 40,000. It is worth a visit if only to see its museums, all of which are in the southern part of the town. The first to be reached is the Museo della Vita e delle Tradizione Popolare Sarde, which is at the edge of the town, on the small hill of Colle di

Sant'Onofrio. Opened in 1976, the museum is excellently appointed in a group of neat, white buildings that surround a central courtyard. The collection was put together as part of a research and documentation project on Sardinian ethnography. The exhibits include: costumes, textiles, jewellery, ornaments, arms, furniture and musical instruments. There are panoramic views from the museum grounds, taking in the valley to the south, Monte Ortobene to the east, and the Sopramonte range to the south-east.

The Civico Museo Speleo-Archeologico, is 300m (328yd) to the north-west, on the corner of Piazza Vittorio Emanuele, which contains a public gardens. The museum has an interesting collection of archaeological finds from local sites, including prehistoric caves and Nuraghic settlements. Of particular interest, is the collection of menhir, pre-historic monumental stones, which are the only ones of their kind so far discovered in Sardinia.

Nuoro's *duomo* is a short walk north-east of Piazza Vittorio Emanuele. Head to the northern end of the piazza, where there is a permanent exhibition of Sardinian crafts, and turn right along Via Bua. This narrow street leads to Piazza Santa Maria della Neve, along one side of which is the *duomo* of the same name. It was completed in 1854 under the architect-friar, Antonio Cano, and is typical of the era, having a neo-Classical façade. It contains a fine seventeenth-century painting of the *Dead Christ* by A. Tiarini, and other paintings by local artists including Bernardino Palazzi, and also Carmelo Floris and Giovanni Ciusa Romagna who painted the *Stations of the Cross*.

Head north of the *duomo*, to Piazza San Giovanni, and continue from here; along Via Grazia Deledda, through the characteristic quarter of San Pietro. After 200m (218yd) the modest, eighteenth-century family home of the writer, Grazia Deledda (1871-1936), is on the right. It is preserved as a museum in memory of Deledda who brought the unfamiliar world of Sardinia to a wider audience in Italy. Amongst her best-known novels is *Elias Portolu*, which was published in 1903. She later went on to win the Nobel Prize in 1926 for her poetic descriptions of Sardinian life. The museum has numerous first editions of her works in a variety of languages, a collection of photographs and prints, and personal objects and belongings.

At weekends, the Nuorese escape the noise and traffic of the town by driving up to Monte Ortobene. This is a well-recommended excursion, although for peace and quiet it is better to go on a weekday. There is a regular bus service from Piazza Vittorio Emanuele, which visitors may prefer to take, rather than making the 8km (5 miles), winding ascent in their own car. On the way, it is possible to make the diversion to the small church of **Nostra Signora della Solitudine**, which is 1 ½km (1 mile) east of the town, on Viale Ciusa. This peaceful spot, at the foot of Monte Ortobene, is often alluded to in Deledda's writing, although in place of the simple seventeenth-century church that the author knew, there is now a more ornate reconstruction which contains a memorial to Deledda. A 20-minute walk from the church, takes the visitor to another church, the Madonna di Valverde. Nearby, there is a fresh-water spring and in the granite rock there are numerous carved recesses, resembling a giant honeycomb. Hewn bedrock such as this is found throughout central Sardinia, but despite this, their origins are uncertain. According to legend they are the houses of fairies, or witches and are hence called *domus de janus*. It is more probable, however, that they are burial grounds dating from the Nuraghic era.

The main road continues to zig-zag up the great granite mass of Monte Ortobene, passing numerous natural springs on the way. At **Farcana** there is a modern sports centre with a heated, open-air swimming pool and a horse-riding school. The road ends at a parking area, from where a track leads to the east side of the mountain. Here stands the giant bronze statue of the Redeemer, 7m (23ft) high, which was erected in 1903 by the sculptor Vincenzo Jerace. The mountain top is criss-crossed by footpaths marked for walkers, and there are numerous picnic areas, as well as restaurants which specialise in barbecued meats.

Route 2b starts at Orgosolo. It is therefore unnecessary to return to Oliena; instead continue south, past the Oliena junction, on the SP58.

Route 2B • Oliena to Fonni

From Oliena, head north for a short distance on the road to Nuoro, before turning off left. This road crosses over a well-cultivated river basin at the far side of which is the junction with the SP58. Turn left at the junction and follow the SP58 for a further 11km (7 miles) along the wide banks of the Locoe river. Shortly, Orgosolo comes into view on the hilltop ahead and the road starts to climb steeply up. Look out for the boulder with the brightly-painted apache, 2km (1 mile) before reaching the village, on a hairpin bend on the right. A short distance further, also on the right, another rock is painted with a lady in a blue dress.

Orgosolo is renowned for its mural paintings. In the centre of the town, there is barely a wall nor building left unpainted. The subject matter varies from historical and cultural themes, to issues, such as emigration and grazing rights. Most have a political message, often reflecting the deep-rooted bitterness that seems to hang in the town's atmosphere. The idea for painting the murals was spawned in the spirit of the 60s when a group of local students and teachers got together with an artist, Pasquale Buesca, from Siena. Amongst the first of the murals to be painted was of a 15 year vendetta over a property dispute, that had started in Orgosolo in 1903. Vendettas, feuds and banditry are all part of Orgosolo's history, although in more recent years it has become somewhat glamorised following the 60s film, *Banditi a Orgosolo*, which was directed by Vittoria di Seta and partly staged in the town.

Most of the murals are concentrated along the main road, Corso Repubblica, and the street parallel to it, Corso Garibaldi. The small carpark at the eastern end of Corso Repubblica, on Piazza Caduti in Guerra, is a good point from which to start a tour of the town. The piazza is named after the war monument at its centre and on one of the surrounding buildings there is a detail, borrowed from Picasso's *Guernica*. While wandering around the town, the visitor will notice that many of the murals are influenced by Picasso. Others follow the Mexican tradition or are painted in a naive style, while the most recent additions tend to be roughly-scrawled graffiti, usually defacing an already existing work. The murals, however, are not permanent, and if they are not painted over, then they quickly deteriorate, as they are done with water-based household paints.

Although Orgosolo is a quiet town, with most of its inhabitants gaining their livings from sheep-rearing, the murals have attracted a certain amount of tourism and there is a handful of restaurants which serve the local Cannonau wines amongst others, and a few souvenir shops selling crafts. Traditional costume is increasingly a thing of the past, but some of the older women still dress in the old way, wearing clothes of a heavy black fabric, with a head covering to match.

Leave Orgosolo by following signs to Mamoiada. For those that wish to explore the wilderness of the hills surrounding Orgosolo, take the first left fork off the Mamoiada road, to **Montes**. The fork leads to the *caserma* (old barracks) which are set in an expansive forest of holm oak. To go hiking in the forests, which are the property of the State, it is necessary to apply for a permit beforehand from the Direzione Foreste Demaniali (see Additional Information at the end of this chapter). From Montes an unmetalled track continues for some 10km (6 miles) to Monte Novo San Giovanni. This remote spot was a popular hideout for the bandits of Orgosolo, and in the more remote past it was most probably the site of a Nuraghic settlement. The views from the peak of Monte Novo San Giovanni, which is

(Opposite) The colourful Festa del Redentore, Nuoro

An unusual sight to see is this painted rock at Orgosolo

Orgosolo is renowned for its mural paintings

1,316m (4,316ft) high, are outstanding.

The route, however, heads westwards along the winding road to Mamoiada, which lies 11km (7 miles) away. The first part of the drive climbs steadily uphill for 7km (4 miles) through a wild and uninhabited landscape where rugged moors and rocky ridges stretch for as far as the eye can see. The summit of the hill is at an altitude of 745m (2,444ft), and after reaching it the road heads downhill, all the way to Mamoiada, which is surrounded by well-cultivated land and vineyards.

✳ **Mamoiada** is a small, rural town dependent on sheep-farming. Due to its remote location in the mountainous interior of Sardinia it is something of a backwater, and it is not unusual to see locals getting about by donkey. However, the town is of national repute for its carnival, which traditionally takes place before Lent, with a warmup version in January to celebrate the festival of St Anthony. The procession, is lead by *mamuthones*, men dressed up to represent the devil. They are clothed in sheepskin and wear gruesome wooden masks and carry clusters of bells (weighing as much as 14kg/30lbs) on their backs. This evocative ceremony has its origins in Pagan times when a similar hunting procession took place in honour of Mars. Today, a similar parade is re-enacted at cultural and folkloristic events throughout Italy, and is a central feature of the carnival in Sassari. The *mamuthones* masks are seen throughout Sardinia, being widely sold in souvenir shops.

While wandering about the narrow, steep streets of Mamoiada, the visitor will notice traces of Roman masonry and stone fragments built into the simple, rustic houses. The most impressive Roman relic
✳ is the Fonte Romani which is signposted from the town centre. It is located on the hill in the old part of the town and is best approached on foot, rather than negotiating the very narrow streets by car. From the main road, head uphill, following the signposts. Bear left whenever in doubt and you will shortly reach the fountain which is on the right. Surmounted by a mock-classical façade, the lower part of the fountain consists of the original stones. Water gushes from two circular spouts into a curved basin, before draining into gutters that carry the gurgling water under the road.

The route continues along the main road, the SS389, south of Mamoiada, in the direction of Fonni, which is 16km (10 miles) away. After winding down through dense forests of oak to the Taloro river, the road heads uphill again and continues through a richly-forested landscape where oak grows alongside chestnut and cork.

Appearing quite suddenly above this rich, leafy canopy, is **Fonni**, which lies along a high ridge at an altitude of 1,000m (3,280ft). It is the highest town in Sardinia and enjoys magnificent views all around. The inhabitants are mostly shepherds and in the winter months they migrate with their flocks to the flat plain of the Campidano. However, as the shepherds depart, skiers arrive, as Fonni is a popular base from which to go ski-ing on Monte Spada (1,595m/5,232ft), one of the northernmost peaks of the great Gennargentu massif. In the summer, hikers use Fonni as a base from which to make the ascent of Punta La Marmora which lies to the south of Monte Spada. It is the highest peak in the Gennargentu and from the summit, on a fine day, it is possible to see the south, west and east coasts of Sardinia. The mountain is named after the French man, Alberto Ferrero de la Marmora who hiked all over the island in the nineteenth century and undertook the first geographical study of Sardinia, recording his journey in the *Voyage en Sardaigne*. For those interested in the ascent of La Marmora, which involves a strenuous 3- or 4-hour trek, head south of Fonni on the road to Desulo for 5km (3 miles), before turning left onto a rough track that leads to the ski lift. The track can be followed for almost 10km (6 miles) to the refuge, which lies at an altitude of (1,570m/5,150ft), at the foot of Bruncu Spina. A ski-lift runs to the peak of Bruncu Spina (1,829m/5,999ft), but it is only in operation during the ski-ing season. The hike therefore begins by climbing Bruncu Spina before heading south, following shepherd's paths, to Punta La Marmora which is 1,834m (6,015ft) high. The trail is marked on the Istituto Geografico Militario maps of Desulo and Punta La Marmora, which are essential, as are suitable clothing and provisions. The hike is only recommended during the summer months as there is snow until May.

Fonni also has a well-attended sanctuary, the Santuario della Madonna dei Martiri. The building dates from the Baroque era and has a good collection of eighteenth- and nineteenth-century paintings and sculptures inside. A pilgrimage is made to the sanctuary on the first Sunday after Pentecost, which coincides with a Spring festival. Fonni has another festival, also religious, on the 24 June. It is dedicated to St John and is well worth attending as beautiful costumes are worn by the local women.

Route 2C • Fonni to Laconi

Route 2c leaves Fonni by following the SS389dir, a narrow and winding road that heads through a spectacular landscape of open hills and dense oak forests. **Gavoi**, which is scenically positioned, high on a hill to the right of the road, is typical of the villages in this region, with its simple houses built of stone. The tall bell-tower which dominates the village is part of the late-Gothic church of San Gavino. The church has a simple façade, pierced by a rose window, with a Renaissance portal below. The wood-carved baptismal font, in the interior, which dates from the seventeenth century is worth stopping for. The village used to be known for founding horses' spurs, and tackle and bits. Now, however, the main craft is textile weaving, both of carpets and cloth.

Continuing along the SS389dir, the road shortly reaches the shores of **Lake Gusana**, a large, man-made basin formed out of the Taloro river. The densely wooded hills that surround the lake make it a spot of great natural beauty. It is remarkably unspoilt, with only one major hotel at the southern end, which not only commands a beautiful view, but has some exceptionally well-placed tennis courts overlooking the water. The waters are stocked with fish, and boating is popular in the summer, although bathing is not recommended. The road crosses a thin arm of the lake, which drains southwards into the Aratu river, before continuing high along the western shore. At the westernmost point, the lake merges with the steep and rocky ravine of the Taloro river, from where there are scenic views.

The hills beyond the lake are densely covered in forests of holm and cork oak. The cork oak (*quercus suber*) is indigenous to this region, although it is maintained and used by man, and has been a major industry since the nineteenth century. Every 8 to 10 years, when the bark is thick and spongy on the outside, it is stripped from the tree trunk, exposing a vivid red-coloured underbark, known as the cambium. Most of it is used to make corks for bottles, although some is utilised in the production of souvenirs. A certain amount is also exported in its raw state.

The next habitation is not reached until **Ovodda**, which is just under 10km (6 miles) from the lake. It is a simple village with rustic houses built of the local grey granite and a small church with a neat stone belfry. From Ovodda, the road winds gradually downwards to another small village, **Triana**, which is picturesquely set in the Tino river valley. The valley marks the north-eastern boundary of the wine-growing region of Mandrolisai. The SS389dir continues into the Mandrolisai wine-growing country, crossing the Torrei river, before climbing up to a road junction, which is some 8km (5 miles) south of Tiana. Here, visitors can make the excursion to the interesting little town of **Sorgono** which is the centre of the Mandrolisai region. The road to Sorgono winds steeply up to the S'Isca de Sa Mela pass, which is at an altitude of 950m (3,116ft), before heading down into a wooded valley. Sorgono lies at the bottom of the valley, at a total distance of 7km (4 miles) from the junction.

A panoramic view towards Lake Gusana

D.H. Lawrence visited Sorgono by train in 1921 and described his approach to the town from the station with elation. '… we seemed almost to have come to some little town in the English West Country, or in Hardy's country. There were glades of stripling oaks and big slopes with oak trees, and on the right a saw-mill buzzing, and on the left the town, white and close, nestling round a baroque church-tower.' His spirits were to be dampened by the prospect of a night in a flea-bitten hotel, but even in his anger and disillusionment he writes of the surrounding hills: 'No denying it was beautiful, with the oak-slopes and the wistfulness and the far-off feeling of loneliness and evening.'

Sorgono still has a limited range of accommodation, but this is part of the town's time-worn charm. The centre is gracefully endowed with large, crumbling *palazzi* which are straggled along the main street. One of the more important of these buildings is the Casa Carta. It is typical of the late Gothic-Aragonese style, having ornate pillars flanking its square windows and portals. According to its inscription it was built in 1606. The Baroque church, referred to by Lawrence, still marks the town's hub, on Piazza della Vittoria. It is reconstructed on the foundations of an earlier Aragonese church, of which only the bell tower, dating from 1580, remains intact. The façade is of an attractive, pink stone, but the interior has been unsympathetically modernised and is only of interest for the wooden crucifix that dates from the Aragonese era.

Perhaps one of the main purposes of a visit to Sorgono, however, is to go to the Cantine Sociale, the main co-operative in the region producing Mandrolisai wines. There are two varieties of Mandrolisai, the *rosso* which is a light, ruby red, best drunk after two or three years, and the *rosato*, a rose which is to be drunk young. The *cantina* is located at the bottom end of the town, on the right of the main street.

The route continues southwards on the SS295 to **Tonara**. This small town lies in a verdant pass, at an altitude of 930m (3,050ft), at the western edge of the Gennargentu mountains. It is well-known for its *torrone* (nougat), which is made with egg-white, honey, almonds and hazelnuts. It is also a productive textile centre. Flat-weaves and pile rugs are made with the local wool and can be found in small workshops such as Co-op Tessile, which is signposted on the left, at the entrance to the town. The Sardinian Institute for Associations of Craft Work, I.S.O.L.A., also have a centre in Tonara, in Via Caralis, where it is possible to watch weavers, as well as buy the products. A good picnic spot, and also a pleasant place to walk in Tonara, is the Sorgente Galuse. This is the site of a natural spring, 2km (1 mile)

above the town, clearly signposted from the centre.

From Tonara, follow signs to Cagliari on the SS289, which continues slowly winding southwards through the foothills of the Gennargentu. After 6km (4 miles) the road joins a broad valley, at the far end of which Belvi and Aritzo can be seen. Before reaching these villages, those keen on hiking in the Gennargentu, may wish to make the 8km (5 mile) excursion off left to **Desulo**. There is a well-trodden shepherd's trail from Sarcu de Tascussi, which is just west of Desulo, up to Bruncu Spina, from where a footpath continues up to Punta La Marmora, the highest of the Gennargentu peaks. The maps necessary for hiking around here are: *Desulo* and *Punta la Marmora*, published by the Istituto Geografico Militario. Visitors should be warned, however, that Desulo has a reputation for lawlessness and camping is not recommended in the vicinity.

The route continues along the Aratu river valley on the SS295 through stunning, wild landscape with wide open views of the majestic peaks of the Gennargentu. The only signs of life are the flocks of sheep whose bells echo across the moors, and the occasional shepherd. The little village of **Belvi** lies at the southern end of the valley, some 8km (5 miles) from the Desulo junction. Belvi is known for its cherries which grow in neat orchards surrounding the village. It also has a museum which is passed on the right on the way out of the village. Known as the Museo Scienze Naturali e Archeologico, this modest museum contains a motley collection of stuffed birds and animals native to Sardinia. These include birds of prey, Sardinian partridges and flamingoes, as well as 4-legged species such as moufflon, boar, deer and wild cats.

From Belvi, the SS295 climbs up above the Uatsu valley to the village of **Aritzo** which lies directly overhead at an altitude of 796m (2,611ft). Surrounded by forests of chestnut and hazelnut, Aritzo has a delightful setting, and commands a fine view of the valley below, with Tonara visible in the far distance. In the summer it is popular as a mountain resort and there are various amenities for tourists, including sports facilities, folkloric events, and organised hiking, horse-trekking and canoeing excursions. The canoeing excursion is one of the most exciting in Sardinia as it involves navigating 6km (4 miles) of the Flumendosa river, where there are challenging rapids, canyons and creeks. The Flumendosa river lies to the south of Aritzo and is one of the major rivers in Sardinia, being 122km (76 miles) long. Further details of organised activities can be obtained from the local *comune* (town hall), the address of which is in the Additional Information at the end of this chapter section.

The centre of Aritzo is marked by the parish church which has a

The harvesting of the cork oak tree

stout bell tower, dating from the fifteenth century. The tower has triple openings at the top and a pointed spire, both of which are typical features of the late-Gothic style in Sardinia. The interior holds a gilded Catalan crucifix which was made by goldsmiths in Cagliari, and two wooden polychrome statues: the one of the *Pieta* is by a local artist and dates from the eighteenth century; the other, of *San Cristoforo*, dates from the seventeenth century and stylistically resembles the work of Bernini.

At the southern end of the village, visitors will find the Parco Communale Pastissu, where there are facilities for sports and hiking. Other good hiking spots are to be found in the surrounding countryside which is well-endowed with natural springs. Two of the more impressive springs, Sorgente Is Alinos and the Sorgente Sant-Antonio, are signposted from the village centre.

From Aritzo, the route continues southwards on the SS295 to Laconi. The road climbs steeply up along a rocky ridgeway which affords dramatic views in all directions. On the left, rising above a pine-forested valley is the village of **Gadoni**. On the right is an imposing chain of rugged peaks, many of which culminate in extraordinary peaks. The road continues to climb through pine and chestnut forests to **Valico Sa Casa**, a mountain pass, at an altitude of 1,040m (3,411ft). From this high and barren pass, the road gradually winds down, passing through the dense forests of Ortuabis. From time to time, one catches a glimpse through the trees of the more gentle hills ahead which gradually flatten out towards Sardinia's southern coast. The last part of the journey is made alongside the narrow-gauge railway which runs from Cagliari through the Barbagia. The road traverses the railway several times and drivers should proceed with caution as the crossings are manually operated. After the first railway crossing, the road follows a spectacular limestone gorge where the sparkling Bidissaru river can be seen far below. The gorge gradually opens out into a forested landscape of gently rolling hills which eventually give way to the Southern Lowlands. The majestic plateau, the Giara di Gesturi, is in the distance, and directly below are the red roof tops of Laconi.

Additional Information

Places to Visit

Belvi

Museo Scienze Naturali e Archeologico
Open: daily.
☎ 0784 629467 (Custodian)

Nuoro

Civico Museo Speleo-Archeologico
Via Leonardo da Vinci 5
☎ 0784 33793
Open: Tuesday to Saturday 9am-12.30pm, 4.30-7pm. Sunday 9am-12.30pm.

Museo della Vita e delle Tradizione Popolari Sarde
Via Mereu 56
Colle di Sant'Onofrio
☎ 0784 37484
Open: winter, Tuesday to Saturday 9am-1pm, 3-6pm, Sunday 9am-1pm. Summer, Tuesday to Saturday 9am-1pm, 3-7pm, Sunday 9am-1pm.

Museo Deleddiano
Istituto Superiore Etnografico
Via Deledda 42
☎ 0784 34571
Open: Tuesday to Saturday 9am-1pm, 3-7pm. Sunday 9am-1pm.

Tonara

I.S.O.L.A.
Sardinian Institute for Associations of Craft Work
Via Caralis
Open: daily 9am-12noon, 3-6pm.

Useful Information

Aritzo

Events and Festivals
Last Sunday October, Sagra delle Castagne e delle Nocciole. (Festival of Chestnuts and Hazelnuts, exhibition and free distribution of local dishes and sweets).

Tourist Information Centre
Comune di Aritzo
☎ 0784 629223

Belvi

Tourist Information Centres
Pro Loco
Viale Kennedy 26

Comune di Belvi
☎ 0784 629216

Fonni

Events and Festivals
Sunday after Pentecost, Sagra della Madonna. (Pilgrimage to Santuario della Madonna dei Martiri, festival of Sardinian dance and song, procession in traditional costume, exhibition of local crafts).

June, Festa di Su Poggione. (Named after the bread that is baked for the festival in the shape of a bird. The main events at the festival are a poetry competition and a procession in traditional costume).

Tourist Information Centre
Comune di Fonni
☎ 0784 57022

Emergencies
Carabinieri (Military Police)
☎ 0784 57001

Gavoi

Events and Festivals
Last Sunday July, Festa di Nostra Signora di Sa Itria. (Shepherd's festival).

Tourist Information Centres
Pro Loco
Via Roma
☎ 0784 534000

Comune di Gavoi
☎ 0784 53120

Mamoiada

Events and Festivals
17 January, Festa di Sant'Antonio.
(Procession of *mamuthones*, people
dressed in traditional wooden
masks with sheep's bells on their
backs. The procession is a less
elaborate version of that below).

Pre-Lent, Sos Mamuttones.
(*Mamuthones*, which is the local
dialect for 'devil', parade through
the town, dressed as above,
accompanied by *issocadore*, men
with lassoes. Spectators caught by
the lassoers have to make a
donation or sacrifice. The parade
ends with the *mamuthones* being
driven out of the town in a
ceremony that symbolises the
dispelling of bad luck).

Emergencies
Carabinieri (Military Police)
☎ 0784 56022

Nuoro

Events and Festivals
Beginning May, Sagra di San
Francesco di Lula. (Religious
festival of St Francis of Lula).

Last Sunday August, Sagra del
Redentore. (Festival of the
Redeemer. The festival was started
in 1901 when the giant bronze
statue of the Redeemer was erected
on Monte Ortobene. A procession
of 3,000 people, dressed in
traditional costume, parade
through the town. The festival ends

with a solemn, religious procession
up to Monte Ortobene).

August, Festivale Regionale del
Folklore. (Regional Folklore
Festival, 50 folk groups compete in
a singing and dancing competition
which is held in the stadium).

Tourist Information Centres
Ente Provinciale per il Turismo
Piazza Italia 19
☎ 0784 32307 or 30083

Comune di Nuoro
☎ 0784 30211

Ufficio Amministrazione Foreste
Demaniali
(Forestry Commission-hiking
permits)
Via Trieste
☎ 0784 35730

Comunita Montana del Nuorese
Via Brigata Sassari 1
☎ 0784 37584

Transport
Maggiore Autoservizi (Car Hire)
Via Convento 32
☎ 0784 30461

Ferrovie dello Stato (Railway)
☎ 0784 30115

Travel Agencies
Ancor
Via Manzoni 85
☎ 0784 30463

La Nuova Barbagia Tours
Piazza Veneto 27
☎ 0784 34579

Viaggi Avionave
Via Lamarmora 117
☎ 0784 37446

Viaggi Granturismo
Via Brigata Sassari 15-17
☎ 0784 36856

Emergencies
Polizia (Police)
☎ 0784 30000

Polizia Municipale (Municipal
Police)
☎ 0784 30212

Carabinieri (Military Police)
☎ 0784 32171

Polizia Stradale (Traffic Police)
☎ 0784 34000

Pronto Soccorso (First Aid Service)
☎ 0784 36302

Ospedale San Francesco (Hospital)
☎ 0784 31091 or 36616

Croce Rossa (Ambulance Service)
☎ 0784 36302

Automobile Club d'Italia
Via Sicilia 39
☎ 0784 30034
NB: Those hiking in the province of
Nuoro should contact the following telephone numbers in case of
forest fire, or if wounded animals
or birds are found:
☎ 0784 35731 or 30122

Oliena
Events and Festivals
Easter, Processione di S'Incontru.
(Procession in local traditional
costume).

End of August, Processione di San
Lussorio. (Procession in local
traditional costume).

Tourist Information Centres
Associazione Pro Loco
Comune di Oliena
Piazza Palach
☎ 0784 287240

Cooperativa Enis
Via Aspromonte 8
☎ 0784 287460

Emergencies
Carabinieri (Military Police)
☎ 0784 287522

Guardia Medica (Medical Officer)
Via Nuoro
☎ 0784 288014 or 287649

Orgosolo
Events and Festivals
15-17 August, Festa dell'Assunta.
(Festival of the Assumption,
celebrated by a procession in
traditional costume, folk dancing
displays, poetry competition, horse
race and Sardinian songs and
dancing).

Tourist Information Centres
Comune di Orgosolo
☎ 0784 402126

Azienda Foreste Demaniali della
Regione Sarda (Forestry Commis-
sion — hiking permits).
Caserma Forestale Montes, Loc.
Funtana Bona
☎ (0784) 402287

Emergencies
Carabinieri (Military Police)
☎ 0784 402122

Guardia Medica (Medical Officer)
Via Sant'Antonio
☎ 0784 402143

3

THE SOUTHERN LOWLANDS

Travelling southwards from Barbagia, one experiences a great contrast in landscape, as the rugged mountains of the interior give way to the vast area of plains and lowlands, that extends to the Mediterranean coast. Chapter 3 traverses this flat expanse, from the southern edge of Barbagia, to the sweeping salt flats that surround Sardinia's principal port and capital city, Cagliari. The route avoids the major roads where possible, as they tend to be dull and monotonous. It is far more rewarding to travel along the quiet country roads, taking in the more remote corners of the region, as well as the major sites of interest.

The attractions of the Southern Lowlands are various. Historically, a great number of Nuraghic settlements were built here in the second millennium BC, and many are still standing. The sites of *Su Nuraxi* and *Genna Maria* are amongst the best-preserved examples of Nuraghic fortresses in Sardinia. Other settlements are left unexcavated, but the hefty blocks of stone, from tumbled walls and fallen towers, that are strewn across the landscape, lend it great character. It is also a region of considerable geographical and geological interest. Ancient volcanic eruptions have left strange conical peaks and prominent table top mountains that stand isolated like islands in the plain. Some are surmounted by fortresses and watchtowers, others are natural havens for local wild life, such as the famous miniature ponies of Sardinia that roam the plateaux of Giara di Gesturi.

The flat, treeless Southern Lowlands are good agricultural land, the most intensely cultivated area being the great alluvial belt, the Campidano, that stretches from Oristano on the west coast, to Cagliari on the south coast. The Romans referred to the Campidano as their 'granary', and built the road from Cagliari to Porto Torres, across the plain, to transport the grain. This road is still the main artery on the island, although it is now called the Superstrada Carlo Felice, after the Savoy King who had it reconstructed in the 1820s. The Campidano plain continues to supply mainland Italy with grain as well as providing the island with most of its fruit and vegetables. The towns spread across the plain are relatively prosperous and several have fine, historic churches and buildings.

Chapter 3 is divided into three sections, all of which can be covered in a relatively short time, due to the flat roads. The route ends at Cagliari, which is the starting point of Chapter 4.

Route 3A • Laconi to Barumini

Laconi is dramatically situated, at an altitude of 555m (1,820ft), at the southern edge of Sardinia's mountainous interior. It is a small town but there is enough of interest to occupy the visitor for at least a morning. The town is mainly of note for its history as a seat of the local nobility. The Laconi Counts, who lived here from medieval times onwards, endowed their town with fine buildings and monuments, many of which are left standing. The town is of religious acclaim, as it is the birth-place of the Capuchin laybrother, Ignazio di Laconi, who was beatified after his death. A fine park, covers the hill above the town, from where the views across the lowlands below, to the great plateau, Giara di Gesturi, are breathtaking.

The central square, Piazza Marconi, is a convenient point from which to start a tour of the town, and holds one of the principal buildings in Laconi, Palazzo Aymerich. This pink, neo-Classical *palazzo* was built in 1846, to a design by the architect G. Cima, for the Marquis of Laconi, who moved here from the medieval residence on the hill above the town. It is now the seat of the town hall and also houses a museum. The museum has a collection of around fifty ancient menhir, prehistoric monumental stones, which date from the third millennium BC. The *palazzo* is complete with its original neo-Classical furnishings, but these can only be viewed on request.

 Leave Piazza Marconi by taking Via Sant'Ignazio from the north-east corner of the square. The house where St Ignazio was born is 50m (55yd) along the first street on the right. It is a modest building with a somewhat decayed exterior, and houses the saint's few meagre possessions inside. The house is well-attended by pilgrims and can be visited by calling on the custodian who lives next door.

Return to Via Sant'Ignazio and proceed a short distance further, to the division in the road. From here, the left branch leads to the parish church, which is topped by a prominent dome and has a fine sixteenth-century bell-tower. Next to the church, which is dedicated to St Ignazio, there is a permanent exhibition illustrating the life of the saint. Ignazio Vincenzo Peis, born of poor village folk, in 1701, was accepted into the order of the Capuchin Franciscans at the age of 20. He spent the next 40 forty years of his life, in Franciscan simplicity, begging alms for the friars' support. He died in 1781 and was canonised by the Roman church in 1951.

The church, which was refurbished in the twentieth century, following Ignazio's canonisation, has two large paintings of interest: the *Ecstacy of St Anthony* and the *Virgin and Child*. Both are typical of the Baroque era and are believed to be by the same artist. There is also a noteworthy, polychrome, wooden statue, decorated with gilt, of *St Anthony of Padua*, which was made in Naples and dates from the eighteenth century.

Returning to the division in the road, take the right branch, Via Don Minzoni, to the town's park. The entrance to the park is at the end of the road, on the left. From the gates, a footpath crosses a gurgling river and enters a jungle-like forest. Lebanon cedars, holm-oaks, eucalyptus, beech, willow and linden form a dense, green canopy overhead, while running water trickles through the undergrowth, providing luscious vegetation all around. The abundance of water comes from the large waterfall at the top of the hill, and from natural springs which are dotted throughout the park. Even during summer drought, this is a verdant spot, while in autumn the dampness provides ideal conditions for fungi. Toadstools and mushrooms of every size, shape and colour can be seen carpeting the ground.

Take any of the footpaths which wind up the hillside to the ruined medieval castle of the Laconi nobility, the Castello degli Aymerich. It was first built in 1053, but underwent reconstruction many times, as can be seen by the odd assortment of relics left standing today. The oldest part of the building is the tower. The principal gateway, which is seventeenth century, leads into a spacious, but roofless hall, dating from the fifteenth century. The hall is typical of Gothic-Catalan architecture of the era, with its ornately-carved, stone windows. The windows on the south-west side of the building command a magnificent view across the plain below, to the Giara di Gesturi plateau. Excellent views can also be had by continuing up the hill, above the castle, to the main waterfall which cascades down the pink-red rock.

The route continues south of Laconi on the SS128 which is signposted to Cagliari from the bottom end of the town. The road gradually winds down, over sparse and barren hills, to the undulating plain below. Ahead, the small volcanic cone of Zeppara Manna

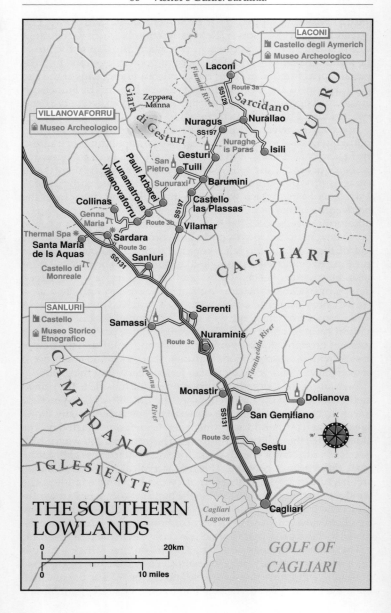

THE SOUTHERN LOWLANDS

GOLF OF CAGLIARI

(580m/1,902ft), marks one end of the vast, basalt plateau of **Giara di Gesturi**. The Giara, which is local dialect for 'plateau', rises prominently from the dark-earthed plain. It is 12km (7 miles) long and has an average width of 4km (2 miles). It is covered in small cork oaks and scrub, and has numerous craters and pools that fill with rainwater in the spring, making it a regular stopover for migratory birds. The most important wildlife on the Giara, however, is the Cavallini della Giara, a breed of miniature wild pony. There are between five and eight hundred of these little ponies, with their almond-shaped eyes, roaming the plateau in semi-wildness. Their existence, however, is constantly threatened. In the summer they have to contend with drought and famine, while in the winter there is ice and snow. They are also hunted by the local farmers who sell them for horse meat or for breeding. The new foals are rounded up in July and August and then branded by the farmers that claim them. Probably, in the future an end will be put to this age-old tradition as there are plans afoot to make the Giara a national park area. In the meantime, visitors to the plateau are very unlikely to catch even a glimpse of these ponies as they tend to inhabit the highest and most remote areas. The Giara is a good walking spot, although there are no marked footpaths and cars can proceed no further than the lower slopes of the plateau.

The Nuraghic fortress, **Nuraghe Is Paras**

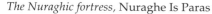

The SS128 heads towards the Giara, passing through the small village of **Nurallao** which is built on a small rise in the plain. At the other side of the village, those that wish to make the excursion to Isili should bear left. The road to Isili follows the broad valley of the River Fiumini which is streaked with low outcrops of limestone and is eerily desolate; the only habitation around here is a penal colony. After a short distance, the road crosses over the River Manna, which is overlooked by a ruined church, and then gently climbs up to the site of a Nuraghic fortress, *Nuraghe Is Paras*. The site is clearly signposted on the right of the road, and stands on a small mound. It has a well-preserved central tower with one of the largest Nuraghic domed tops in Sardinia.

The road continues a short distance beyond *Nuraghe Is Paras* to the village of **Isili** which covers a small hillock, at a height of 523m (1,715ft) above sea level. Follow the signposts straight ahead to *centro*, where on the left of the main street, the visitor will see the typical Sardinian church of San Giuseppe Calasanzio. The church is shaped like a bee-hive, with an ample terracotta-tiled dome and a white-painted façade. The interior stands on a circular ground plan and is of interest for the unusual granite pulpit which dates from the seventeenth century. Isili is reputed for its handicrafts, and produces a wide range of textiles, such as bedspreads, bags and carpets, and also copperware, all of which can be found in the local shops.

Returning to Nurallao, the route continues towards the Giara on the SS197. The road traverses a wide open expanse of plain, where there is little to see except for the occasional circular sheep pen and mile after mile of dry-stone walls. After 3 ½km (2 miles) the road passes through the village of **Nuragus**, which stands on a site that was inhabited in both the Nuraghic and Roman eras. As testimony, there is a Nuraghic well just outside the village, and in the parish church, the font is made from a Roman milestone.

The SS197 continues to the slopes of the Giara which are cultivated with olive groves and vineyards. The village of **Gesturi** lies on the south-eastern slope of the Giara, commanding a fine view across the plain. Visitors who wish to see the Giara ponies kept in captivity should turn right at Gesturi and follow signs to Giara di Gesturi Cavallini. The route, however, continues to the village centre, where there is a fine parish church, built of an attractive, pink stone with a tall, decorative bell tower. Beyond Gesturi, the SS131 heads downhill, towards the village of Barumini, the red rooftops of which can be seen in the plain below.

Route 3B • Barumini to Villanovaforru

Barumini is mainly visited for the famous Nuraghic site of *Su Nuraxi* Ͳ
which lies nearby. However, the village itself is also worth stopping
in, as it has an interesting church at its centre. Built in 1541 in the late-
Gothic style, it has a prominent dome and an elegant belfry that is ⅄
typical of the era. The interior is also typically Gothic, with pointed
arches along the aisles and vaulted ceilings. In the choir, which is
surmounted by a cupola, there is a Gothic altar-piece which is made
up of a statue of the *Assunta* with painted panels behind, by the
Cavaro school. Also of interest is the fifteenth-century, carved altar
step which is preserved in the sacristy. It is beautifully decorated
with figures of the Apostles and was done by the Gothic-Catalan
school. Nearby the church, look out for the Casa Marchionale, a ▦
sixteenth-century *palazzo*, built for the noble Zappata family. Its
windows are particularly attractive and are carved from stone in the
Renaissance style.

Su Nuraxi, one of the best-preserved Nuraghic fortresses in Sar- Ͳ
dinia, is 1km (½ mile) east of Barumini on the road to Tuili. The site
is clearly signposted from the village outskirts, and is easily visible
on the left of the road. The carpark is also on the left, just before the
site entrance.

Archaeologists have dated the earliest remains of *Su Nuraxi* from
the fifteenth century BC, although additions and modifications were
continuously made, up until the invasion of the Carthaginians in the
sixth century BC. Until 1949, the ruins lay hidden beneath a mound
of earth, which, it is speculated, may have been intentionally placed
to camouflage the site from the Romans. Howsoever, the earth
preserved the fortress in excellent condition, and only revealed what
lay inside when it was partly washed away in a flood. Excavation of
the site has taken place ever since and even now the archaeologists
are still at work, although the restoration of the central fortress is now
complete.

The fortress is believed to have been part of a line of defences that
guarded the hinterland from coastal invasion. However, it is somewhat grander than other defence encampments and it is thought that
it was probably also the seat of a local ruler. Built with massive blocks
of dark, basalt stone, without the use of mortar, it has a tall, circular
tower at its centre, which is surrounded by bastions and walls. The
tower, which is the oldest part of the fortress, dates from the fifteenth
century BC. It was originally 21m (69ft) high and had three storeys.
Today, it still stands to an impressive 15m (49ft) with two of the
storeys intact. A modern staircase has been attached to the east side
of the tower in order to preserve the original stairs, which spiral

around inside the thick walls. The staircase leads up to a small, circular room on the second floor which has a conical roof and a window. The window looks down into a courtyard where there is a well at the centre.

To explore the rest of the fortress, follow the footpath around the base of its walls. At each of the four points of the compass, there is a circular defense tower, which were added to the central tower in the ninth and eighth centuries BC. An additional wall with further defences was built in the sixth century BC. The ruins to the east of the fortress walls, near the site entrance, are the remnants of a village. Some fifty circular houses have been uncovered, as well as evidence of a bakery which has a mill for grinding the grain, kneading basins and large ovens. The mill-stones that were found in the mill are of an impressive size, with a diameter of some 2m (7ft). Most of the ruins in the housing quarter date from the eighth century BC, but as it was later used by the Carthaginians and Romans there are subsequent additions. The later houses, added in the fourth and third centuries BC, tend to be eliptical rather than circular in ground plan. The entire quarter is connected by a complex system of alleyways and steps, and although only the lower parts of the walls are left standing, one is left with an evocative impression of how a Nuraghic village must have looked.

Looking across the plain from *Su Nuraxi*, the visitor will probably have noticed an unusual, conical-shaped hill on the horizon. It is called the Mamella (Bosom) after its shape, and is topped by the ruins of a twelfth-century castle. Las Plassas, as it is known, was built on the border between the former territories of the judiciaries of Arborea and Cagliari, respectively, which ruled the area during the medieval era.

From *Su Nuraxi*, visitors short of time may wish to drive directly to Cagliari on the SS197 via Vilamar. Route 3b, however, continues to dawdle across the plain, exploring an area known as the Marmilla, which is typified by the humps and rises that unexpectedly protrude from the bleak flatness. The first stopping point on the Marmilla plain is **Tuili**, which is a short distance further east of *Su Nuraxi*. This small village lies on the southern slopes of the Giara and has two interesting churches. The more important of the two is the church of San Pietro, which stands on a small piazza at the top of the village. It has a rather severe and gloomy exterior, but inside, in the first chapel on the right, is one of the greatest works of fifteenth-century,

(Opposite) Su Nuraxi, *one of the best preserved fortresses in Sardinia, Barumini*

Sardinian art, the *Retablo di San Pietro*. A *retablo*, or retable, is the back of an altarpiece, traditionally composed of a series of painted wooden panels which are set within a frame. It is a format particularly common to Spain, which is no coincidence, as the *Retablo di San Pietro* was painted in 1500, when Sardinia was ruled by the Aragonese.

The Aragonese, turning their backs on the Renaissance movement that was then flourishing on mainland Italy, brought artists to Sardinia from the Catalan School. Sardinian artists were thereafter obliged to follow in the style of the Catalan School, although their work retained a Sardinian spirit. The fusion of the Catalan and Sardinian styles is clearly exemplified in the *Retablo di San Pietro*. Attributed to the anonymous Sardinian painter, the Maestro di Castelsardo, the *Retablo* is made up of two large central panels, flanked by two smaller panels at either side and a predella, composed of seven very small panels, along the base. The lower central panel depicts the *Madonna and Child with Angels*; and the upper show the *Crucifixion*, which is attended by groups of pious women and soldiers. On the left side, the bottom panel is of *St Peter*, and the top panel of *St George*. On the right side, the top panel depicts *San Giacomo*, and the bottom panel, *St Paul*. The panels are framed by a decorative Gothic surround which is also painted. In many aspects it resembles the polyptyches painted in medieval Tuscany, particularly those of the Sienese School. At the same time it has the Gothic decorative detail, prevalent in the fifteenth- and sixteenth-century Catalan Schools. It was this very decorativeness that the Spanish found lacking in Sardinia's art and architecture, particularly when it came to the adornment of family chapels, such as the one in San Pietro.

The other church in Tuili, Sant'Antonio Abate, is also a monument to the Spanish era, although it dates from the eighteenth century which was the latter end of their rule. It is positioned on the right hand side of the main road through the village, and is a good example of the Spanish Baroque in Sardinia.

The villagers in Tuili are renowned for their skill at capturing the Giara ponies, and in August, a festival is held, during which the ponies are branded. It may not appeal to everyone, but it is an ancient tradition that is not intended as cruel sport. Tuili also has a well-stocked *enoteca* (wine shop) with a good selection of the local wines.

From Tuili, head south across the treeless plain towards the primitive, agricultural village, **Pauli Arbarei**. There are fine views to the left of Castello Las Plassas, crowning its conical hill, while to the right, rises the small table plateau of Pranu Siddi. A short distance beyond Pauli Arbarei, the road meets a crossroads, at which point visitors should continue straight over to **Lunamatrona**. This large village, like so many on the Campidano plain, is centred around its church. Built of an attractive, warm-coloured stone, Lunamatrona's church, the Chiesa San Battista, was built in the sixteenth century along with its neat, stone belfry.

From Lunamatrona, follow signs to Villanovaforru, which lies a further 6km (4 miles) south. The landscape here undulates in a series of dips and hummocks. The soil is stony and vegetation is sparse, there being only the occasional olive grove, vineyard or almond orchard. The road gently climbs up to Villanovaforru which lies at an altitude of 324m (1,063ft) and is the starting point of Route 3c.

Route 3C • Villanovaforru to Cagliari

Villanovaforru has become an increasingly popular tourist centre over recent years due to the unearthing of the nearby Nuraghic settlement, *Genna Maria*. The village has two or three souvenir craft shops, a handful of restaurants, and a well-appointed museum, the Museo Archeologico, which contains finds from the Nuraghic excavations. The museum, in a small piazza at the village centre on the left hand side of the main road, is housed in an attractive *palazzo* with a neo-Classical façade. The exhibits are well-displayed on two floors of the *palazzo*. On the ground floor, in a spacious, stone vaulted room, there are large, earthenware storage jars and other ceramic vessels, as well as bronze implements and saddle-shaped millstones, all of which were found in the living quarters of *Genna Maria*. On the first floor, at the top of the stairs there is a scale model of *Genna Maria*, which gives a good idea of how the settlement must once have looked. The collection of archaeological finds here, however, are from other Nuraghic sites in the Marmilla region. Most of the exhibits were found near the surface of the earth and are therefore less well-preserved than the finds from *Genna Maria*. However, there is also a collection of Punic and Roman objects, which are better-preserved, including items of jewellery and numerous oil lamps.

To visit *Genna Maria* (keep the museum ticket for entry to the site), follow the main road out through the village. Turn left onto the road to Collinas, and then left again up a small road, signposted to the *complesso nuragico*, which climbs up to a carpark at the foot of the hill on which *Genna Maria* stands. Proceed on foot, from the carpark, up the steep track to the hill summit. There are panoramic views in all directions. On a clear day it is possible to see both the gulfs of

Oristano, to the west, and Cagliari, to the south. To the south-west the Campidano gives way to the Iglesiente mountain range, and to the north-east one can see across the Marmilla to the Giara plateau.

The fortress of *Genna Maria*, which crowns the very top of the hill, dates from the second half of the second millennium BC. Like the fortress of *Su Nuraxi*, it has a fat central tower, surrounded by bastions and fortifications. It is not possible to go inside the fortress, as restoration work is still underway. However, a footpath makes a circuit of its walls and should be taken in an anti-clockwise direction, which is the order in which the information boards are arranged. The central tower, constructed with megalithic blocks of white stone, is the oldest part of the fortress. It is surrounded by bastions and three other towers with narrow slit windows, which were added at the end of the second millennium BC. Further walls, to strengthen the towers and bastions, were added in the ninth century BC. Surrounding the outer fortress walls are the ruins of a village. The houses are mostly circular and are built with much smaller stones than those used in the construction of the fortress. The main concentration of housing is on the east side of the hill where the great majority of finds in the Villanovaforru museum were discovered. During the excavations, evidence was found of a fire which partially destroyed the settlement and coincided with its abandonment in the eighth century BC. It was never to be inhabited again and lay buried beneath the earth up until twenty years ago. It was, however, used as a place of worship during both the Punic and Roman periods.

From *Genna Maria*, resume the main road to **Collinas**, an attractive village with a fine church built of yellow-coloured stone. After Collinas the road gradually winds down, over gently undulating hills that are cultivated with vineyards, olive groves and almond orchards, to the Campidano plain. **Sardara**, which is just over 5km (3 miles) south of Collinas, lies on the gentle slopes bordering the eastern edge of the plain. It is a simple, but attractive old town with many fine belfries punctuating its skyline. One of the most notable churches in the town is that of San Gregorio which stands on a small square at the town centre. It was built in the thirteenth century and is typical of the Romanesque style then common in Sardinia. Its façade is decorated with arcades and bands of yellow stone, and it has a ponderous, square belfry at one side. From San Gregorio, follow Via Eleonora for 500m (564yd), to another of Sardara's pretty churches, Sant'Anastasia. The church is on the right hand side of the street and has a simple façade with an elegant open belfry. It stands on the site of an ancient Nuraghic spa which was supplied with curative waters from a spring that rises nearby. All that remains of the spa is an underground pit of a former temple which dates from the tenth century BC. The spring water was carried by pipe to this limestone and basalt-lined pit which could be entered by a staircase. The pit is now closed off, although you can get permission to see it by applying to the local *comune* (town hall). Excavations in and around the pit have yielded a large collection of ritualistic implements made from clay. They are particularly finely-crafted, decorated with symbols, and are believed to date from the eighth century BC. They can now be seen in the Cagliari museum.

Sardara is still an important centre of natural spring water, and 4km (2 miles) west of the town there is a well-known thermal spa resort at **Santa Maria de Is Acquas**. The resort, Terme Santa Maria, ❊ is modern, although it occupies the site of the most antique spa in Sardinia. It is joined to a large hotel, Hotel delle Terme. The waters have the highest levels of bicarbonate of soda to be found in Italy and

Villanovaforru

are used in the treatment of liver disorders and digestive problems. Treatment takes the form of massages and curative beverages, and last for twelve to fourteen days. There are also thermal baths where the water feeds from the ground at around 50°C (122°F).

From Sardara, the route proceeds along the main highway on the island, the SS131, or Superstrada Carlo Felice as it is more commonly known. At the junction with the SS131, to the south-west of Sardara, the visitor will see the ruins of **Castello di Monreale**, a squat fortification, crowning an isolated mound at the edge of the Campidano plain. Turn left onto the SS131, which follows alongside the eastern edge of the plain, in the direction of Cagliari. The next place of interest, **Sanluri**, is 8km (5 miles) along the road, on the left. Follow the yellow signs through the outskirts of this large, agricultural town to the *castello*, which stands at the centre of Sanluri, on the right hand side of the road.

The castle was built in the fourteenth century as the seat of the Cagliari judiciary. When the Aragonese took over Cagliari and its territory, the castle at Sanluri was the setting for the signing of a peace treaty with the neighbouring judiciary of Arborea. However, peace was not to ensue, and in 1499 the Arborese lost their independence in the battle of Sanluri, at the hands of Martin II of Aragon. Today, the castle is restored as a private residence, but the apartments of General Villa Santa are open to the public (see Additional Information at the end of this chapter for times).

The castle stands on its original square ground plan with a neat turret at each of its four corners. The walls are rendered with plaster, which takes away its medieval character, but the original corner stones have been left and some of the arrow slits remain in the lower walls. It is surrounded by fir trees, set in neatly-kept gardens which hold a collection of World War II anti-aircraft and anti-tank guns. The entrance to the castle is along the right hand side of the building. Inside, the apartments, which are decorated in the style of the Napoleonic era, contain various collections, including some autographed verse by the poet Gabriele d'Annunzio and wax figurines. There is a collection dedicated to the Duke of Aosta made of memorabilia from the two World Wars and Mussolini's war in Ethiopia.

Back outside the castle, on the opposite side of the street, a small road leads up to a Capuchin monastery which houses the Museo Storico Etnografico. Also of interest, is the church of San Rocco, which is passed on the way. It dates from the sixteenth century, and was built under the Aragonese, in the Gothic style. Before leaving Sanluri, the visitor may wish to sample the local bread, for which the town has a widespread reputation. It is made with the grain grown on the Campidano plain and kneaded into giant-sized loaves which are baked in wood-fuelled ovens.

From Sanluri, head back to the SS131 and continue towards Cagliari which is a further 35km (22 miles) south. The road follows the gently undulating Campidano plain which is richly cultivated with grain, vines and olive trees. A series of towns are passed on the way. **Serrenti**, 10km (6 miles) south of Sanluri, is a centre of tufa mining and many of the houses around here are built with the local stone, which is known as Pietra di Serrentu. **Nuraminis** is surrounded by market gardens, while **Monastir**, another agricultural town, is attractively positioned on a rocky outcrop overlooking the Flumineddu river.

Those interested in Romanesque and Gothic architecture may wish to make detours along the way to the numerous historic churches that are dotted around the area. At **Samassi**, which is 6km (4 miles) due west of Serrenti, there is a fine, thirteenth-century church, dedicated to San Gemiliano. The exterior walls are decorated with typical Romanesque arcading and pilaster strips. The interior, which is made up of a single nave, holds the beautifully-carved, sixteenth-century mausoleum of Don Giacomo of Castelvy, a Knight of St James. Another Romanesque church can be visited at **Dolianova**, which lies 15km (9 miles) due east of Monastir. The façade of the church is decorated with blind arcades and carved with figures and animals, reminiscent of eastern stone masonry. The eastern influence on Romanesque architecture is also seen at **San Gemiliano**. This small village, and church of the same name, is reached by turning left off the SS131, just before reaching Sestu. It was constructed in the thirteenth century by Arab stone masons who embellished the structure with many eastern style decorations. Unfortunately, the church underwent enlargement and modifications in the sixteenth century with the addition of a portico and sacristy. However, the original structure is still discernible in places.

After passing the town of **Sestu**, which is 10km (6 miles) south of Monastir, the industrial developments of Cagliari start to appear. The roads become increasingly busy with traffic and their are a series of intersections and traffic lights. The city centre can either be reached by following the *centro* signs, or those to the *porto*. The latter route is probably less frantic, and leads the visitor into the city alongside the Cagliari lagoon.

Additional Information

Places to Visit

Barumini
Nuraghe Su Nuraxi
Open: winter daily 9am-4pm. Summer daily 8am-1 hour before sunset.

Laconi
Museo Archeologico
Palazzo Aymerich
Piazza Marconi ☎ 0782 869578

Sanluri
Castello ☎ 070 9307105
Open: winter Sun 3-5.30pm. Summer Tue, Wed and Fri 4.30-8pm.

Museo Storico Etnografico
Convento dei Frati Cappuccini
☎ 070 9371147 Open: Mon, Wed & Fri: 9.30-12 noon 4-6pm.

Sardara
Terme Santa Maria
Santa Maria de is Acquas ☎ 070 934025
Open: April to November.

Tuili
Enoteca Zonca Fulvio (Wine)
Piazza Umberto 17 ☎ 070 9364021
Open: Mon to Sat 8am-12 noon, 3-7pm.

Villanovaforru
Museo Archeologico
Viale Umberto I ☎ 070 9300048
Open: winter, Tue to Sun 9am-1pm, 3.30-5.30pm. Summer, Tue to Sun 9am-1pm, 3.30-5.30pm (same ticket for Genna Maria).

Genna Maria
Complesso Nuragico. Open: winter, Tue to Sun 9am-1pm, 3.30-5.30pm. Summer, Tues to Sun 9am-1pm, 3.30-5.30pm.

Useful Information

Barumini
Events and Festivals
22-23 May, Sagra della Tosatura. (Sheep-shearing Festival.

Dolianova
Events and Festivals
First Sunday after Easter, Sagra di Pasqua. (Easter festival, 3 days of musical events & religious processions).

Laconi
Emergencies
Carabinieri (Military Police)
☎ 0782 869022

Guardia Medica (Medical Officer)
Via Romaora
☎ 0782 869013

Sanluri
Tourist Information Centre
Associazione Pro Loco Via Carlo Felice

Travel Agencies Neltourist
Via Umberto 19 ☎ 070 9307026

Emergencies
Carabinieri (Military Police)
☎ 070 9307012 or 9307022

Polizia Stradale (Traffic Police)
☎ 070 9307028

U.S.L. (Medical Care) Via Carlo Felice
☎ 070 9307224 or 9307225

Sardara
Emergencies
Carabinieri (Military Police)
☎ 070 9387022

Guardia Medica (Medical Officer)
Via Fontana Nuova ☎ 070 9387263

Tuili
Emergencies
Guardia Medica (Medical Officer)
Via G.B. Tuveri 13 ☎ 070 9364030

Villanovaforru
Emergencies
Carabinieri (Military Police)
☎ 070 9367722

Guardia Medica (Medical Officer)
Via Venezia-Villamar ☎ 070 9309011

4

THE SOUTH-WEST

Chapter 4 starts at Sardinia's capital city, Cagliari, and finishes in the foothills of the Iglesiente, where mining has taken place for almost 3,000 years. In between the two, is one of the most beautiful of Sardinia's coasts, which is characterised by red, rocky cliffs and idyllic sandy bays. The coast is studded with the romantic ruins of trading colonies, dating from the early Phoenician era, and numerous watch-towers that were built to guard against Saracen invasion.

For nature-lovers, there are plentiful lagoons and marshes where flamingoes, herons and cormorants are just a few of the birds that can be spotted. The wine-lover will find plenty of interest in the coastal region of Sulcis. The wines produced here are mainly dry reds that are best drunk when young and are made from the Carignano grape, a variety that is usually only grown in France and Spain.

Just offshore from the Sulcis coast, is a volcanic archipelago which includes the two large islands of Sant'Antioco and San Pietro. Tuna fishing is one of the main sources of income on these islands, and the visitor will find tuna dishes feature prominently on most restaurant menus. This includes *bottarga*, the eggs of tuna fish, which is the Sardinian equivalent of caviar. A small jar of *bottarga* makes a good souvenir to take home. Lobsters are fairly common too, as are eels and mullet which are drawn from the inland lagoons. In Cagliari, one of the fish specialities is *Sa Burrida*, filleted catfish with a walnut and liver sauce, cooked in olive oil, white wine and garlic.

The route is divided into three sections, each of which requires at least two days. For overnight stays, Cagliari has a reasonable selection of accommodation, although most hotels and campsites are to be found along the coast to the east of the city, in and around Poetto. Travelling west of Cagliari, the numerous beach resorts all have accommodation facilities too. For top class luxury, there are several hotel complexes around Santa Margherita di Pula, which are second only in opulence to those on the Emerald Coast. There are also a good number of campsites dotted amongst pine forests along the beaches, although the further from Cagliari one travels the less developed the coast becomes.

Route 4A • Cagliari

Cagliari, the capital of Sardinia, is the largest, the busiest and the most industrialised city on the island. It has been the capital since Roman times, making it one of the oldest in Europe, although the city's origins actually go back much further. *Karalis*, as it was first named, was established as a Phoenician trading colony, being excellently-positioned on the east-west Mediterranean trade route, and having a wide and sheltered natural harbour within the Golfo degli Angeli. The Carthaginians, the Romans, and later the Pisans and Spanish, were all to prosper from the city's links with maritime trade, just as the modern city does today. It is the island's most active harbour and the seventh largest port in Italy, and is crowded with cranes and cargo vessels.

Despite Cagliari's industrial might and its unsightly surburban sprawl, the city centre is full of character. There are picturesque, narrow streets, chic boulevards lined with palm trees, and a gracious historic centre, known as Castello, which is contained within an impressive citadel wall. Cagliari's monuments span the wide and varied course of its history, from ancient Roman ruins through to the affluent era of the House of Savoy. The majority of these monuments are within a compact area, in and around the citadel, and can be tackled quite comfortably on foot with enough to keep the visitor occupied for at least a day or two.

Visitors arriving in Cagliari by car are well-advised to stow their vehicles away as soon as possible. The city traffic is hectic, parking is impossible, and unfortunately car theft is rife. It is recommended to book into a hotel with a secure carpark, or leave your car in a private garage, of which there are a number dotted around the centre. For daytime parking, there is a large custodian carpark at the port, however, be warned that it closes at sunset.

The centre of Cagliari lies a few hundred metres inland from the port, around the prominent limestone hill on which the citadel stands. Largo Carlo Felice is the principal boulevard leading from the port to the base of the citadel mound. On the corner of this street, overlooking the port, is the startlingly white **Palazzo Comunale** which has a façade like an iced cake, pierced by dozens of windows and surmounted by twin towers. Built in 1897 for the House of Savoy, it is a typical neo-Gothic creation, although it is closer to the contemporary architecture of the Aragonese, rather than to that of Piedmont, which is perhaps not surprising as the Spanish dominated Cagliari for some 400 years. The interior, which is now used for council meetings, is also richly decorated, and contains a number of fine paintings by sixteenth-century Sardinian painters such as Cavaro and Figari, as well as Flemish artists. The paintings are hung in two of the grandest rooms: the Sale dei Matrimoni (the Wedding Chamber) and the Salone dei Ricevimenti (the Banqueting Hall).

At the opposite end of Largo Carlo Felice is a statue of the Piedmontese, King Carlo Felice, who commissioned numerous monuments in the city, as well as public works such as the road from Cagliari to Porto Torres which in Roman times ended right here. Beyond the statue, is a pleasant square surrounded by trees, the Piazza Yenne, which is named after the Marquess of Yenne who was married to the Sardinian Viceroy, Ettore Veuillot. Head uphill, through the piazza, towards the great tower that looms overhead, **Torre dell'Elefante**. This excellently-preserved construction was built after the Pisans took control of the city and guarded one of the two principal entrances to the citadel. It is a remarkable structure, being assembled of huge blocks of stone, without the use of mortar. It was designed in 1307, by Giovanni Capula, and stands to its original height of 30m (98ft), along with an awe-inspiring section of the citadel wall which is also built with great blocks of skilfully-cut stone. It takes its name from the small, stone-carved elephant that protrudes from the wall to the left of the portcullis. Just inside the citadel walls, to the right is the university, the Universita degli Studi, which was founded during the Spanish period of rule, under Philip II, in 1605. It was in the Physics Department here, in 1875, that the dynamo was invented, by Antonio Pacinotti.

The tour continues by proceeding straight ahead, beyond the Torre dell'Elefante, and on up the hill through the narrow alleys and stairways that characterise this old medieval quarter of the city. Eventually, the tangle of small streets open out onto a piazza, full of parked cars, at the far side of which is the cathedral.

Cattedrale Santa Maria was built by the Pisans in 1312. Its façade, typical of the Pisan-Romanesque style has blind arcading and geo-metric medallions decorating the lower walls, and three layers of dainty colonnades stacked above, which culminate in a high central section. The three simple portals are set between pilaster strips and have mosaic-decorated lunettes above each. However, only the robust belfry to the left of the façade is original, the rest is a faithful

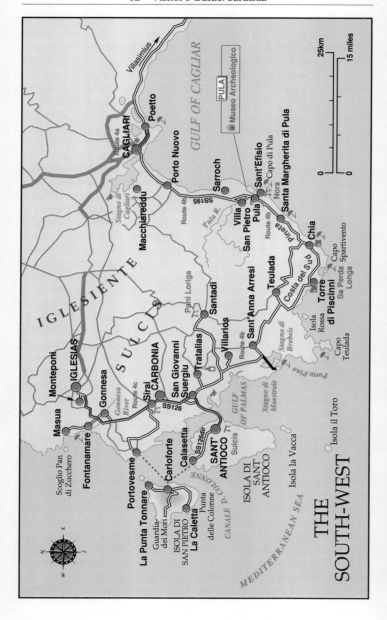

Palazzo Comunale in Calgliari

reconstruction that was undertaken in 1933.

The interior of the cathedral, has not been restored to its Roman-esque appearance, and is predominantly Baroque, with lavish, inlaid marbles covering the walls and ornate frescoes decorating the ceil-ing. One of the only remaining original features is the pair of stone-carved pulpits that stand at either side of the main door. Each pulpit, supported on four columns, is beautifully-carved with animals and figures, as well as deep reliefs depicting scenes from the New Testament. The pulpits, presented to Cagliari as a gift by the cathe-dral in Pisa in 1312, were made by the Pisan stonemason, Maestro Guglielmo, in 1159. Guglielmo also made the four stone lions that sit on the raised presbytery, each with a different animal held between its front paws. The presbytery is enclosed by a fine seventeenth-century marble balustrade, while below it, marble steps lead down into a sanctuary which was hewn from the natural rock in 1618. There is not a trace of rock to be seen, however, as it is entirely clad in white and blue stucco work. The arched ceilings are studded with white stucco rosettes and diamonds, said to number 600 in all, and the walls are lined with stucco niches with a saint depicted in each one. The niches, of which there are 292, were to hold the relics of early Christian martyrs and Sardinian saints that were found below the church of San Saturno (see below).

Back outside, head north of the cathedral, through Piazza Palazzo, passing the **Prefetura** on the right, which was built in 1769 as the Savoy residence. Inside, there is a grand assembly chamber, deco-rated with allegorical frescoes by Bruschi, and an elegant staircase which was designed by De Guibert. Continue uphill, along Via Martini, where there is a good viewing terrace on the right. Perched high above the east walls of the citadel, the view takes in the eastern part of the city and the coast beyond, including Capo Teulada which encloses the eastern end of the Golfo degli Angeli, and the inland marshes and salt-pans of Molentargius and Quartu. Via Martini ends, after a short distance further, at Piazza Independenza. In the north-east corner of this piazza is **Torre San Pancrazio**. This vast tower was built to guard the second of the principal entrances penetrating the citadel walls, and was designed by the same architect as the Torre dell'Elefante, in 1305.

The other dominant feature in Piazza Independentza is the bright pink building which houses the **Museo Archeologico Nazionale**. Constructed in 1800 by order of Charles Felix of Savoy, it has a typical neo-Classical façade, even if its colour breaks somewhat from tradi-tion. The main door leads into a circular vestibule; the ticket office is on the right and the entrance to the first salon is on the left. The first salon contains a fascinating collection of finds from Nuraghic settlements in the region, the most important of which are a series of bronze figurines, displayed in the cabinets on the right. Dating from 800 to 600BC, they are thought to have been votive statues, as most were found in sacred caverns and wells, temple precincts and cult places. Each one is a unique work of art. Characters are depicted from all walks of life: archers with bows and arrows; sovereigns wearing capes; warriors with swords and horned helmets; shepherds; athletes; mothers suckling; and also boats which have animal heads decorating their sterns, and were probably used as votive lanterns. Analysis was carried out in the United States, where thousands of these figurines have been clandestinely exported, to determine the actual make-up of the material. The results proved that the figurines were definitely made of bronze, being composed of 80-90 per cent copper and 10 per cent tin. The proportions varied slightly, however, and up to 0.5 per cent arsenic, 0.5 per cent lead, 0.3 per cent zinc and 0.3 per cent iron, were sometimes also present. The foundries where these bronzes were cast also produced weapons, including spear heads and arrows, the moulds for which can be seen in the same show cases.

The large pieces of statuary fragments in the centre of the room were also found at Nuraghic sites and date from the seventh century BC. The small figurines, carved from bone, in the display cabinets on the left side of the room, were found in a *domus de janus* (witches' houses), near Alghero and depict female cult goddesses.

Return to the circular vestibule and take the door on the right into the second salon. The collection of archaeological finds here, ranges from the Phoenician era which started in the first millennium BC, to the second century BC which saw the end of Carthaginian rule and heralded the beginning of the Roman era. Of particular interest from the Phoenician era, are the inscription stones dedicated to the deity Sid, that were found at the temple of *Antas* (see Route 5). Dating from the Punic era is a rare, painted tomb found at *Sulcis* (see Route 4c) and many tophets, small funerary stelae belonging to children. There is also some fine black and red pottery of Carthaginian origin. In the third salon, there is a wide range of exhibits dating from the late Carthaginian era up until Roman times. There is a good collection of Roman, clay figurines and votive heads which are from the fourth to second century BC. There are also numerous pieces of Roman glass, oil lamps, as well as a number of anonymous marble busts, dating from the second and first centuries BC.

From Piazza Independenza, continue to head north, passing through the archway to the left of Torre Pancrazio, into Piazza

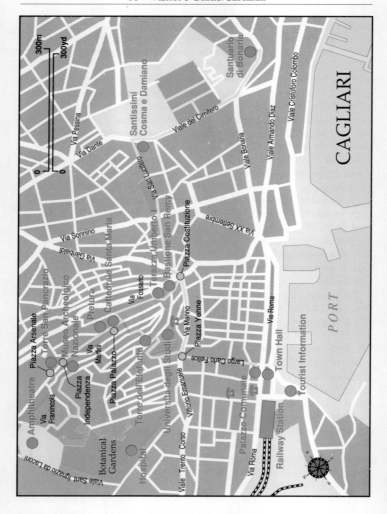

Arsenale. This small piazza is at the highest point of the citadel and is surrounded by the buildings of the former arsenal. The city's museum collections are scheduled to be re-housed in the arsenal, but restoration work progresses but slowly.

Head through the arch on the left of Piazza Arsenale and proceed downhill, along Via Franincola, from where a good view can be had

Relax at a pleasant street café in Via Roma, Cagliari

Bastione San Remy and Piazza Costituzione, Cagliari

through the railings of the remains of the Roman **Amphitheatre**, the best edifice of its kind in Sardinia. It is only possible to go inside the amphitheatre when there is a performance, so the visitor may well content themselves with the view from here. The theatre is hewn from the natural rock, and although the seating is badly eroded, its size alone is impressive. According to Pliny it could seat some 20,000 spectators in its day, which constituted the entire population of the city. It was constructed in the second century and was used for gladiatorial and animal spectacles. The pits where the animals were kept can still be seen beneath the stage.

Those that wish to visit the **Botanical Gardens**, should proceed on down the hill, passing around the north side of the Amphitheatre, to the entrance to the gardens which is on Viale Sant'Ignazio da Laconi, on the left. The botanical gardens, which belong to the university, were founded in 1865. They cover an area of 5 hectares (12 acres) and contain over 500 species of tropical plants as well as characteristic Mediterranean plants indigenous to Sardinia and Corsica.

The tour of Cagliari continues by heading back through Piazza Independenza, to the cathedral, from where Via Fossario continues southwards. This narrow street, lined with tall *palazzi* along either side, ends at the vast panoramic terrace, **Terazza Umberto I**. The view from the terrace is quite breathtaking; it encompasses almost the entire city, embraced by its lagoons, and the Golfo degli Angeli, from Capo Teulada to Capo Terra. The terrace is built atop the southernmost bastion of the citadel, known as **Bastione San Remy**. San Remy was the first Piedmontese viceroy to rule Sardinia after the 400-year Spanish domination. He commissioned the enlargement of the citadel walls during his reign, but it was the Piedmontese King Umberto I who had the monumental staircase built which leads down from the southern side of the terrace. This grandiose marble staircase, which dates from 1899, leads down to Piazza Costituzione, a busy traffic junction. Cross over to the west side of the piazza and follow Via Manno, which is Cagliari's main shopping street. Lined with smart clothes shops, Via Manno is the main parading spot in the city, and around sunset you will find all the best-dressed people in town walking up and down here. The street ends at Largo Carlo Felice, near Piazza Yenne, which was the starting point of the tour.

There is little else of major interest in the city. However, those interested in early Christian churches, may wish to head out to **Santissimi Cosma e Damiano**, also known as San Saturno, after Saturnus who was martyred here during the reign of Diocletian (AD284-305). It is located in a modern part of the city, just under a kilometre to the east of Piazza Costituzione. Only the shell of the building remains with its shallow central dome supported on four arches. It was built in AD470 which makes it the oldest and most important Christian monument in Sardinia.

Another church, **Santuario di Bonaria**, lies 650m (710yd) to the south of Santissimi Cosma e Damiano, atop a monumental flight of steps. It was built in 1325 and still has its Gothic portal, although the rest of the building is Baroque. The church is dedicated to a revered image of the Madonna, which according to legend, was washed up on the shore nearby in a chest from a shipwreck in 1370.

A popular excursion from Cagliari is to the beaches at **Poetto**, a 10-minute drive to the east of the city on the SS125. The 10km (6 miles) of sandy beach here are packed with parasols and bathers throughout the summer. Funfairs, bars, restaurants, beach shops and hawkers are everywhere, and every type of watersport is available. The developments tend to spread a little further along this stretch of the coast each year. However, the further east one travels, the rockier and less suitable for building is the terrain. Away from the crowds, the visitor can enjoy a scenic drive along the cliff tops, which are punctuated with seventeenth-century, Spanish watch-towers, to Capo Carbonara and the attractive, nearby town of **Villasimius**.

Route 4B • Cagliari to Tratalias

Route 4b heads west of Cagliari along the coast, following the SS195, which is signposted from the city centre, to Pula and Nora. At the city outskirts, a long bridge crosses the **Stagno di Cagliari**, an expansive lagoon, which despite pollution and land reclamation, is still a popular nesting ground for marsh birds, including quite rare species such as the Mediterranean slender-billed gull, the little tern, the common tern, the gull-billed tern and the avocet. Amongst the more common species are marsh harriers, black-necked grebes and cormorants which vie with the fishermen for the catch. The most distinguished guest is, however, the flamingo. They arrive during the autumn in flocks of thousands and are a memorable sight as they wing their course across the city. The **Stagno di Santa Gilla**, which lies along the west side of the Stagno di Cagliari, is less well-endowed with wildlife. It is one of the most endangered areas of marsh in Sardinia, due to the extensive land reclamation which has altered the biological equilibrium, and the high pollution levels. The number of ducks and coots that formerly wintered here is decreasing every year.

As the SS195 continues along the coast, industry dominates the landscape. There are large refineries at **Macchiareddu**, nearby

was built in 1291, under the Arborean, Mariano II, along with a city wall that has long since disappeared. The gate is complete with its original, rusticated stone base and crenellations along the top. To the south of Porta Manna, the pedestrianised street, Corso Umberto, is where the town's smartest shops and best-dressed people are to be found. It is lined with chic boutiques and once-grand *palazzi*, and eventually opens out onto **Piazza d'Arborea.**

This narrow piazza is named after the local heroine, Eleonora d'Arborea, whose statue, erected in 1881, stands amongst the palms in the centre of the square. The Arborea family, originally of Catalan descent, were amongst the most powerful rulers of medieval Sardinia. Their judicial territory, which corresponds roughly with that of the present-day province of Oristano, was the last to submit to Aragonese rule. The protagonist of this resistance was Eleonora, who was the *giudica*, from 1383 to 1404. Eleonora also made history by the publication of the Carta de Logu, a code of law, first formulated by her father, which was to serve Sardinia up until 1860. Her statue includes a scroll of the Carta de Logu, which originally had around 200 chapters, held in her left hand.

Leave the piazza from its western end, following Via Sant'Antonio to the neo-Classical **Church of San Francesco**. Built in 1838, the church was designed in the style of the Pantheon, with a broad shallow dome of slate. The dome is most impressive from inside where it is clad in stucco coffering. The building is otherwise unremarkable except for the Spanish crucifix which is set on a stone-carved altar on the left. Painted on wood, it is known as the *Cristo di Nicodemo*, and dates from the fifteenth century.

Take Via Duomo, south of San Francesco, to the spacious piazza that surrounds the cathedral. The **Cathedral** façade forms an attractive corner, along with a seminary, the Seminario Tridentino, and the church of Santissimi Trinita, all of which are Baroque, and date from the eighteenth and nineteenth centuries. Despite its Baroque appearance, the *duomo* was first built in 1228. The only surviving feature of the original structure, however, is the Cappella del Rimedio, which is in the right transept of the interior. The chapel has a fine, stone-vaulted ceiling and an attractive altar made up of Roman pieces of masonry, as well as a balustrade, carved with Pisan reliefs. The interior also holds a medieval, wooden statue of the *Annunciation*, in the first chapel on the right, by the fourteenth-century sculptor, Nino Pisano. Also dating from the fourteenth century, is the *campanile*, standing on the brick terrace, at the back of the cathedral and reached by taking the door from the left side of the main apse. The tower is topped by an onion-shaped dome, patterned with coloured tiles.

Oristano also has an interesting museum, the **Antiquarium Arborense**. This is located in Via Parpaglia, which is to the east of Piazza d'Arborea, in the Palazzo Parpaglia. It houses a good collection of finds from the Classical site of *Tharros*, as well as other artefacts, ranging from Nuraghic bronzes to Carthaginian glassware. The museum also has a painting collection, which contains works by Sardinian masters of the sixteenth century, including a section of a *retablo* which was painted by Pietro Cavaro for the church of San Francesco.

Wine-lovers will be interested to know that Oristano is the centre of production of one of Sardinia's most unique wines. Vernaccia di Oristano, as it is known, is a sherry-like wine, made in a traditional manner, which requires at least two years to complete. The *superiore* and the *riserva* are top of the range, and are aged in wooden barrels, for 3 and 4 years respectively. The result is a very dry, strong wine with a faintly bitter taste. It is served locally, ice-cold as an aperitif. There are also fortified versions of the wine, *liquoroso dolce* (sweet) and *liquoroso secco* (dry), which are very rich and strong. The local cuisine is also worthy of mention, with *bottarga* (mullet caviar) available as a first class accompaniment to the Vernaccia. Fish is a common dish owing to the proximity of the coast and lagoons, and *arragosta* (lobster) is popular in the local restaurants and *trattorie*. Vegetarians will find plenty of variety in the different types of bread that are baked locally and there is also a good local cheese ravioli. Those with a sweet tooth will find the *amaretti* and other almond-based pastries irresistible.

Route 5C • Oristano to Bosa

Route 5c heads west of Oristano to the coast, on the SS292, which is signposted to Torre Grande and Cabras. Keep in the left hand lane, and fork left after crossing the River Tirso. A short distance from the main road, at the pretty, stone church of Santuario del Rimedio, visitors should fork left again, and continue along the bamboo-lined banks of the River Tirso, which is the longest river in Sardinia. After a few kilometres turn right onto the SP3 to **Cabras**, which lies at the edge of a vast lagoon, the **Stagno di Cabras**. A large-domed, six-teenth-century church, dedicated to Santa Maria, with a façade and bell tower of black, basalt stone, presides over this otherwise modest village, which is largely dependent on the fishing of eels and mullet. The lagoon, which lies at the west side of the village, is considered one of the most important natural wetland areas of Europe. It covers an area of some 2,000 hectares (4,820 acres) and is inhabited by great numbers of gulls, cormorants, ducks, egrets and coots.

The route follows along the southern shores of the lagoon, on the road to Tharros, passing the turning left to **Marina di Torre Grande**. This short excursion off the route takes the visitor to the closest beach resort to Oristano. The resort is well-positioned at the northern end of the Oristano Gulf and has a marina as well as a fine beach. The marina, which lies alongside the beach, is one of the most modern in Sardinia and can hold up to 780 boats.

The route continues along the shores of the lagoon, from where there are fine views across to Cabras with its church. After passing a defense tower that was built by the Spanish in the seventeenth century, there is another lagoon, the **Stagno di Mistras**, on the left. The road follows along the shores of this salt-water lagoon, where, during the autumn migration season, it is possible to see flamingoes. Ahead, is the distinctive promontory of **Capo San Marco**. The watch-tower on the tip of this promontory marks the southernmost point of the **Sinis Peninsula**, a region that is steeped in history.

A ruined Nuraghic tower, testimony to the peninsula's early history, is passed to the right of the road, before reaching the village of **San Giovanni di Sinis**. Do not miss the Paleo-Christian church, dedicated to San Giovanni di Sinis, on the left, at the village outskirts. The church dates from the fifth century, and although it is rather unprepossessing from the outside, with its oddly-shaped domes clad in concrete, it is amongst the oldest churches in Sardinia and has an impressive interior. Constructed of large blocks of stone, many of which were removed from ancient *Tharros*, there are three aisles divided by irregular arches, and a robust barrel-vaulted roof. A shallow dome covers the transept crossing, and in the main apse there is a stone-carved altar with a pair of arched windows above.

The village of San Giovanni di Sinis is composed of a motley collection of shacks and huts, which are scattered amongst the sand dunes, at the neck of Capo San Marco. Some of the huts are made of reed, as are the traditional-style fishermen's boats. In the summer, a few bars and restaurants open up in the village, catering for the tourists that pass through here on their way to the ruined city of *Tharros*, which lies a short distance beyond the village, at the tip of the promontory.

Along with *Nora*, this is one of Sardinia's finest Classical sites, and is memorable for both its striking coastal setting and the dramatic, dark, basalt stone used in its construction. The ruins derive from different periods in the city's history. The earliest remains date from the Phoenician era, while Carthaginian and Roman buildings have been superimposed. The city was inhabited up until 1070, at which

Reed huts are found throughout the sand dunes at San Giovanni di Sinis

time, Saracen raids forced the inhabitants to move inland, to the more sheltered position of present-day Oristano.

The road from San Giovanni di Sinis, ends at a parking area, on the left side of which, is the principal north-south artery through the city, the Cardo Maximus. It is one of the best-preserved of the city's ancient roads, being complete with its dark, basalt paving slabs and central drainage channel. The ticket office, from where guided tours depart at regular intervals, is also on the left. Follow the footpath from here, to the remnants of a water cistern, which is positioned at a crossroads. On the hill, to the right of the crossroads, is a Spanish watch-tower. In Carthaginian times, the hill was crested by a fortress and temple, but only very scant relics remain of these. The footpath continues ahead, past a well-preserved section of paved road on the left, to the Roman baths, which are built on a spur of land at the southern end of the city. Broken down walls of brick and stone are all that remain of the baths, but this does not detract from their magnificent setting, perched above a crystal-clear sea.

Return back through the city, along the east coast of the promontory, to the pair of stark, white columns, which are all that is left, to give any real idea of *Tharros'* former grandeur. Dating from the Carthaginian era, the columns belonged to a temple. They are fluted and are intact with their stucco finish, although only one has its original capital. It is difficult to make out the jumble of ruins that are scattered around these columns: they include the relics of other temples, Roman baths, and to the north there are the scant remains of a medieval church dedicated to San Marco. The hill, just inland from here is the site of a Phoenician tophet, or burial ground. Similar to that of *Sulcis*, urns containing the ashes of infants were discovered here in crevices and rock-hewn niches in the natural rock. The urns are now in the Cagliari museum and there is little to see on the hill itself, apart from the remnants of a Roman temple which was built to the south of the burial ground.

From *Tharros*, head back along the promontory, where there are fine, sandy beaches at either side. There are more peaceful beaches, however, to be found along the Sinis peninsula. To reach this part of the coast, return to Stagno di Mistras, and turn left to **San Salvatore** which is passed to the right of the road. This abandoned village's claim to fame is that it was used as the setting for numerous Spaghetti Westerns, including *A Fistful of Dollars*. The dusty, central square is surrounded by simple shacks, and in one corner there is a church with a wooden porch, which is built on the site of an ancient Nuraghic sanctuary. Once a year, pilgrims attend a week-long festival here, during which time they live in the village houses and devote themselves to prayer. The festival culminates in a race with the statue of San Salvatore, from Cabras to the church here.

The route continues north of San Salvatore, along the Sinis peninsula, passing through a flat and desolate landscape where there are fields and fields of thistles and artichokes. After a short distance, it is possible to make an excursion to the coast by taking the left turn to **Is Arutas**. The beach here is made up of dark grains of natural quartz and looks across to the off-shore island of **Mal di Ventre**. As there is no coastal road, it is necessary to return to the inland road, which proceeds up the peninsula, along the western shores of the Cabras lagoon. Beyond the lagoon, the remnants of a Nuraghic settlement are passed, before another excursion can be made to the coast, by turning left to **Mari Ermi**. The beach, which also has tiny grains of quartz mingled in the sands, lies in the shadow of the high cliffs of **Capo Sa Sturaggia**. The cape juts out, roughly midway along the Sinis peninsula, and is a protected nesting ground for cormorants.

Continuing northwards for 6km (4 miles), another excursion to the coast can be made by taking the left fork to Putzu Idu. The road passes by the temporal lagoon of **Sale Porcus** which dries up in the summer, leaving a dazzling white deposit of salt on the ground. In autumn, the lagoon receives thousands of flamingoes, on their migratory route from Africa, to the Camargue in France. Some 9 to 10,000 have been recorded at any one time, which constitutes about 15 per cent of all flamingoes in the Western Mediterranean. Other birds that can be seen on the lagoon, include the crane, the shelduck, the greylag goose and vast numbers of sandpipers. The wildlife of Sale Porcus is protected by LIPU, the Italian League for the Protection of Birds.

Putzu Idu is the only coastal resort of any size along the Sinis peninsula. The beach is made up of soft, white sand and slopes gently to the water, making it a suitable place for children to swim.

From Putzu Idu, follow the road back, past the salt lagoons, to the junction with the SS292. Turn left, and head north of the Sinis peninsula, past the remains of a Nuraghic site, *Nuraghe Tradori*, which covers a mound to the right of the road. The landscape remains rather flat and severe, until it reaches the foothills of Monte Ferru, an extinct volcano with a summit, 956m (3,136ft) high, which the road skirts around in an undulating fashion. From the hilltops there are fine views of **Is Arenas**, the largest sand beach in Italy. It is enclosed by the headland, **Capo Mannu**, at the southern extremity, and **Torre su Puttu**, standing guard at the northernmost end. The latter watch-tower, built of crumbling white stone, is passed on the left as the road joins the coast.

Tharros, *one of Sardinia's finest Classical sites*

The paved road at Tharros, a marvel of ancient engineering

The ruins at Tharros include relics of temples

To the north of Torre su Puttu, around **Sa Archittu**, holiday homes are spread along the coast, while in the bay, just off the main beach, there are the ruins of a wrecked ship. Known as the *Scogli Genovesi* (Genoese Rock), the ship is thought to have sunk about 500 years ago. Those with a dinghy and diving equipment, will be able to explore the debris of the ship with the remnants of its canons, as well as a nearby, underwater grotto. Diving equipment and dinghies can be hired in Sa Archittu (see Additional Information at the end of this chapter).

From Sa Archittu, the road climbs up to a hilltop, 52m (171ft) above sea level, from where a track leads to the right for 3km (2 miles), to the archaeological site of *Cornus*. The remains of this Carthaginian, and later Roman, colony are scant, but it is possible to distinguish the remnants of the acropolis and also an aqueduct.

From the junction to *Cornus*, the road heads down to the coastal resort of **Santa Caterina di Pittinuri** where a large, round tower guards the headland. The headland encloses a narrow bay, around which the resort is neatly arranged. At the centre of the resort, there is a bridge which crosses over the neck of the bay. The road leads up from here, above the bay, past the numerous, white-painted chalets that dot the hillside and command fine views. Continuing along the foothills of the Monte Ferru for 15km (9 miles), the road eventually winds up the olive-covered hill slopes to **Cuglieri**, where some of Sardinia's best olive oil is produced. The town, positioned in the lee of the craggy peak of Rocca Sa, was the scene of the Roman conquest over the combined Carthaginian and Sard forces. Although there are no ancient relics to be seen today, the town has an attractive basilica. Positioned at the top of the town, it has a wide façade, constructed with the dark, local stone, which is flanked by twin bell towers at either side. The same dark, grey stone is used in the construction of the local houses, lending the town a rustic character. A short excursion can be made from Cuglieri, to see the scant remains of **Castello Casteddu Ezzu** which are 3½km (2 miles) along the road to Macomer, on the right.

From Cuglieri, the road winds down, offering fine views of the coast, before reaching **Sennariolo**. Positioned on the left of the road, this small village is surrounded by olive groves and vineyards. It has an attractive church at its centre with a distinctive bell tower, topped by an onion-shaped dome. The road continues to head downwards, crossing over the narrow valley of the River Mannu, before climbing up again to **Tresnuraghes**. As its name suggests, this village stands on the site of a Nuraghic settlement which had three Nuraghic towers guarding its perimeter, of which the remains of one can still be seen in the town centre. To reach the centre, take the sharp left turn which is signposted, *centro*, off the main road. As well as the tower, there is also a fine church which dates from the seventeenth century here. It is topped by a generous, terracotta-tiled dome, and has a façade decorated with pilasters of red trachyte. To the right of the façade stands an elegant *campanile* which has an onion-shaped dome. The interior of the church has a central aisle with chapels recessed along either side, and nineteenth-century frescoes decorating the ceiling.

From Tresnuraghes, the route continues through the hills to **Flussio**, which is 3km (2 miles) away. This small village still produces basketware which is woven in the traditional style with asphodel. The baskets are sold in the local shops along Via Nazionale, the main street through the village. The slopes around Flussio are covered in vineyards that provide the grapes for the prized dessert wine, *Malvasia di Bosa*. The wine is made in Flussio and can be bought directly from the Malvasia di Bosa Cantina Sociale, which is passed on the right of the road.

Flussio runs into the next village, **Tinnura**, where a little, painted church, dedicated to Sant'Anna, is passed on the right. A short distance beyond Tinnura, the road by-passes the small, modern town of **Suni**, at which point visitors should turn left onto the SS129bis. The road heads down into a picturesque valley, which has neat terraces of olive groves along either side. After passing **Modolo**, a small village on the left side of the valley, a series of wide bends take the visitor down into the much larger valley of the Temo river. On the slope overlooking the river is **Bosa**, the starting point of Chapter 6, with its brightly-painted houses and impressive castle crowning the hill.

Additional Information

Places to Visit

Arborea

Centro Ippico (Horse Riding Centre)
Centro Vacanze Ala Birdi
Strada a Mare 24
☎ 0783 801083
45 Anglo-Arabian-Sard horses.
1-2 hour horse-riding excursions,
1 week trek on horseback, horse
riding lessons.

Fluminimaggiore

Museo Paleotologico
Via Sant'Antonio
☎ 070 820197

Iglesias

Museo di Mineralogia
Istituto Tecnico Minerario
Via Roma
☎ 0781 22502
Viewing by appointment only.

Oristano

Antiquarium Arborese
Palazzo Parpaglia
Via Parpaglia 37
☎ 0783 791262
Open: winter daily 9am-12noon,
3.30-5.30pm. Summer daily 9am-
12noon, 4.30-7pm.

Tanca Marchese

Cantina Isola (Wine)
Via Loc. Tanca Marchesa
☎ 0783 82262

Terralba

*Cantina Sociale del Campidano di
Terralba* (Wine)
Via Marceddi 166
☎ 0783 81824

Tharros

Tharros
Open: daily 9am-1pm, 4-7pm.
Guided tours daily 9am-1pm, 3-
6pm. Postcard and bookshop.

Useful Information

Arborea

Emergencies
Polizia (Police)
☎ 0783 800230

Ospedale (Hospital)
☎ 0783 800239

Pronto Soccorso (First Aid)
Service-summer only
☎ 0783 48555

Buggerru

Tourist Information Centre
Associazione Pro Loco
Via Marina 10

Emergencies
Carabinieri (Military Police)
Via Roma 21
☎ 0781 54022

Guardia Medica (Medical Officer)
Via Diaz
☎ 0781 54007

Cabras

Events and Festivals
23-25 May, Sagra del Muggine.
(Fishermen's festival and procession at sea in traditional fishing
craft made of reeds. *Muggine* are
local fish, similar to mullet).

First Sunday September, Corsa dei
Pescatori Scalzi. (Thirty men make
a 6½km 4 miles run from Cabras to
San Salvatore, dressed in white and
bare-footed, carrying the statue of

San Salvatore. The event is a re-enactment of the day in 1506 when the saint was saved in this way from Saracen raiders).

Tourist Information Centre
Pro Loco
Piazza Eleonora 4
☎ 0783 290827

Cuglieri
Events and Festivals
5 August, Festa di Santa Maria della Neve. (Festival in honour of Santa Maria della Neve).

Emergencies
Guardia Medica Turistica (Medical Officer)
Via Regina Margherita
☎ 0781 39599

Iglesias
Events and Festivals
Holy Week. (Hooded procession and Spanish origin rites).

Transport
Ferrovie dello Stato (Railway)
☎ 0781 42041

Travel Agents
Agenzia di Viaggi
Plaisant
Piazza Sella 7
☎ 0781 23564 or 23996

Agenzia di Viaggi
Sulcis Tourist Sud
Via Roma 52
☎ 0781 22690 or 24204

Tourist Information Centre
Pro Loco
Palazzo Civico
Piazza Municipio ☎ 0781 22880

Emergencies
Carabinieri (Military Police)
☎ 0781 42501

Ospedale (Hospital)
☎ 0781 40605

Automobile Club d'Italia
Piazza Gorizia 6
☎ 0781 23435

Marina di Torre Grande
Events and Festivals
15 August, Ferragosto. (Procession at sea).

Emergencies
Pronto Soccorso (First Aid Service)
Summer service for tourists.
☎ 0783 22022

Oristano
Events and Festivals
Last Sunday of Carnival and Shrove Tuesday, Sartiglia. (Horseback contest, including trials and jousting, and traditional game in which riders must spear a metal star with a lance as they ride along. Contestants wear medieval costume and white masks that are of Spanish origin. Takes place on Piazza d'Arborea).
September, Mostra dell'Artiganato e Rassegna Gastronomica. (Crafts and Gastronomy Fair).

Tourist Information Centres
Ente Provinciale per il Turismo
Via Cagliari 278
☎ 0783 73191 or 74191

Pro Loco
Vicolo Umberto 15
☎ 0783 70621

LIPU (Bird Protection Association)
Via Parpaglia 12
☎ 0783 70473

Transport
Contini (Car Hire)
Via Masones 18
☎ 0783 73489

Fara Viaggi (Car Hire)
Via Othoca 72
☎ 0783 72883

Lombardi (Car Hire)
Via Carmine 7
☎ 0783 78289

Taxi
Piazza Roma
☎ 0783 70280

A.R.S.T. (Bus Service)
Via Cagliari
☎ 0783 78001

Ferrovie (Railway)
☎ 0783 72482

Travel Agencies
Sardatur
Via Mazzini 8
☎ 0783 74307

Tharros Viaggi
Via Cagliari 268
☎ 0783 73389

Alerica
Via De Castro 59/61
☎ 0783 300203

Emergencies
Polizia Urbani (Town Police)
☎ 0783 71005

Polizia Stradale (Traffic Police)
☎ 0783 71133

Pronto Soccorso (First Aid Service)
☎ 0783 74261

L.A.V.O.S. (Ambulance Service)
☎ 0783 78222

Ospedale San Martino (Hospital)
Via Fondazione Rockfeller
☎ 0783 74261

Automobile Club d'Italia
Via Cagliari 50
☎ 0783 212458

Sa Archittu
Sports Facilities
Malu Entu (Diving Equipment and
    Boat Hire)
Via dell Alloro 2
☎ 0785 38352

San Salvatore
Events and Festivals
First Sunday September, Festa di
San Salvatore. (Pilgrimage week
culminating in the Corsa dei
Pescatori Scalzi. See Cabras).

Santa Giusta
Events and Festivals
14 May, Santa Giusta. (Four day
festival celebrating patron saint
with services held in church of
same name).

20 April, Regata dei Fassonis.
(Sports and folklore festival).

Tourist Information Centre
Pro Loco
Via Giovanni XXIII

Emergencies
Carabinieri (Military Police)
☎ 0783 359222

Terralba
Emergencies
Polizia (Police)
Via Marceddi 3
☎ 0783 81822

Guardia Medica (Medical Officer)
Via Concordia 12
☎ 0783 816269

L.I.V.A.S. (Ambulance Service)
☎ 0783 81275

Tresnuraghes
Tourist Information Centre
Pro Loco
Via Roma 159
☎ 0785 35563

6

THE UPPER WEST COAST

Chapter 6 continues to travel northwards, along Sardinia's west coast, before heading across the north-westernmost corner of the island, to the city of Sassari. The upper coast is more mountainous and rocky than the lower part, and although there are fewer expanses of flat, sandy beach, the scenery is quite outstanding. The mountainous terrain has delayed the development of the tourist industry and the visitor can enjoy the scenery in all its natural splendour. The starting point of the chapter, the town of Bosa, like the surrounding landscape, is unspoilt, and has a lot of genuine character, as well as many fine buildings and a massive fortress. The next town along the coast, Alghero, is by contrast one of the most popular resorts in Sardinia. From Alghero, the last section of the chapter, Route 6c, is optional. It travels to Sassari via Porto Torres, one of Sardinia's most important ports. However, visitors may prefer to head directly from Alghero to Sassari, which is the starting point of Route 7a.

Amongst the gastronomical delights there is the Spanish cuisine of Alghero, and its famed lobster. The route also travels through the reputable Vermentino wine-making region which is spread between Alghero and Sassari. This white wine is typically dry when young, but sweetens with age. Amongst the best Vermentino is that made by the major wine-producers Sella and Mosca, whose estate can be visited and is included in Route 6c of this chapter.

A day can easily be spent covering each of the three sections of the chapter, although two days is probably necessary in Alghero, if the excursion is made along the headland of Capo Caccia. Allow plenty of time for the journey along the coast from Bosa to Alghero, as the road is narrow and winding, and be sure to set out with a full tank of petrol, as there are no fuel stations on the way.

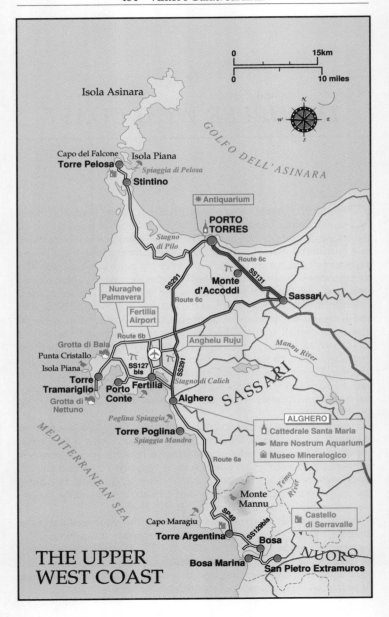

Isola Asinara

GOLFO DELL'ASINARA

Capo del Falcone   Isola Piana
Torre Pelosa
Spiaggia di Pelosa
        Stintino

✳ **Antiquarium**

PORTO TORRES

Stagno di Pilo

Route 6c
SS131

Monte d'Accoddi
                    Sassari

Route 6c

Nuraghe Palmavera

Fertilia Airport

Route 6b   Anghelu Ruju

Mannu River

Grotta di Baia
Punta Cristallo
Isola Piana   SS127 bis
Torre Tramariglio   *Stagno di Calich*
    Porto Conte   **Fertilia**
Grotta di Nettuno   **Alghero**

SS291

SASSARI

Poglina Spiaggia
Torre Poglina
Spiaggia Mandra

MEDITERRANEAN SEA

ALGHERO
▢ Cattedrale Santa Maria
🐟 Mare Nostrum Aquarium
🏛 Museo Mineralogico

Route 6a

Temo River

Monte Mannu

Castello di Serravalle

SP49

Capo Maragiu
Torre Argentina   SS129bis   **Bosa**

NUORO

Bosa Marina   **San Pietro Extramuros**

THE UPPER WEST COAST

Bosa, situated on the bank of the River Temo and surmounted by Castello di Serravalle

Route 6A • Bosa to Alghero

The picturesque town of **Bosa** lies on the right bank of the River Temo, at the foot of a small hill, which is surmounted by the rambling walls of Castello di Serravalle. The oldest part of Bosa, known as Sa Costa, covers the lower slopes of this hill, while the rest of the town is spread alongside the river. Those approaching from the south, on Route 5c, will enjoy the best views of the town, which are to be had from the opposite side of the valley, as the road heads down to the river bed. Before crossing the river, take the turning on the right, to visit the church of San Pietro Extramuros. The road follows the left bank of the river, passing the pink, stone chapel of Sant'Antonio. The chapel dates from the sixteenth century and has a Catalan-Gothic rose window set into its simple façade. The valley here is quite narrow, and the steep olive-covered mountain slopes provide an idyllic setting for San Pietro Extramuros, which is a total of 1km (½ mile) from the bridgehead. Once a cathedral, San Pietro Extramuros was built in at least three different stages, between the eleventh century and the end of the thirteenth century. The oldest parts of the building are Lombard-Romanesque in style, while later alterations show the influence of French-Gothic architecture, a style that was brought to Bosa by the Cistercian monks who established two convents in the town. The façade, which dates from the late thirteenth century, is typically Cistercian. It has three large, pointed arches, with corresponding quatrefoil windows, and a small, decorative canopy crowning the apex. Above the main door, there is an attractive, white, stone architrave which is decorated with naive carvings representing: Saints Peter and Paul, the Madonna and Child, and Costantino de Castra, who was the founder of the church. The big, square *campanile* and the apse were also later additions and date from the twelfth century. Some of the stones used in the construction of the apse, have Pagan inscriptions, and were taken from the Roman necropolis that originally stood on this site.

From San Pietro Extramuros, proceed across the bridge and turn left onto Via Lungo Temo, where parking spaces can be found alongside the promenade. Shaded by a row of stout palm trees, the promenade is overlooked by gracious, eighteenth and nineteenth-century *palazzi*, while on the opposite side of the river are the disused warehouses of Sas Conzas. The warehouses date from the eighteenth and nineteenth centuries, and up until 30 years ago, were used for curing leather. Plans are underway to convert the warehouses to carpenters' and boat builders' workshops.

At the eastern end of Via Lungo Temo, opposite the bridge, is Cattedrale Immacolata. Crowned by a colourfully-tiled dome with a lantern, the building dates from the fifteenth century, although it was largely re-styled in the nineteenth century to a design by Salvatore Are, who looked to the contemporary Piedmont-Baroque architecture for inspiration. The *campanile* and details of the façade are worked in attractive, pink trachyte stone. The interior has ornate, Baroque altars along either side of the central aisle, and a wealth of frescoes by Emilio Scherer, who worked in Bosa in the late nineteenth century.

From the façade of the Cattedrale, head due west along the high street, Corso Vittorio Emanuele II. This narrow, cobbled street is lined with tall, eighteenth-century *palazzi* which have wrought iron balconies and peeling façades, coloured amber and rose. The street leads into the spacious square, Piazza Costituzione, which is also surrounded by elegant *palazzi*, amongst the grandest of which is the eighteenth-century Palazzo Don Carlos, on the northern side.

From Piazza Costituzione, head uphill towards the castle, following the network of narrow alleys through the medieval quarter of Sa Costa. The houses in this district have tall façades, two or three-storeys high, but due to the steepness of the hill, they are only one storey high at the back. The main ascent can be made by the steps, Scala Castello, which lead up from Piazza Carmine. Along one side of this piazza, is the church, Chiesa del Carmine, which was built in 1799, in the same Piedmont-Baroque style as the Cattedrale. Alternatively, visitors can drive up, following signposts to *castello*. The entrance is reached up a flight of steps which lead from Via Nino Gavino.

Castello di Serravalle was founded in 1112 by a noble family, the Malaspina dello Spino Secco, who came to Sardinia in 1016, along with Genoan and Pisan forces, to liberate the island from the Arabs. Hence, this great fortress was built, with its extensive walls enclosing an area of 10,000sq m (11,960sq yd). However, the Malaspina family gradually lost their might, both in Sardinia and on mainland Italy, where they had formerly held power in Liguria, Tuscany and Emilia-Romagna, and the castle was taken by Mariano Arborea who sold it in 1323 to the Aragonese for the sum of 8,000 florins. Under Aragonese domination, the town enjoyed special privileges, and experienced a period of liberty and prosperity. In the nineteenth century, the fortress was a seat of the House of Savoy, and from 1807 to 1821 Bosa was a provincial capital.

Today, the most impressive part of the castle, are the walls with their towers and bastions. The tallest tower, built of light-ochre, trachyte stone, was built in the thirteenth century and guards the keep. Located in the northern corner, the keep occcupies an area of

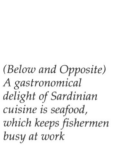

The Cistercian façade of San Pietro Church, Bosa

(Below and Opposite) A gastronomical delight of Sardinian cuisine is seafood, which keeps fishermen busy at work

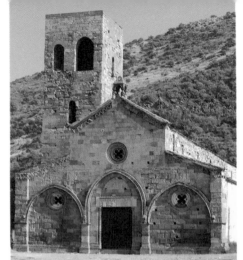

2,000sq m (21,517sq ft), but only the outlines of its walls remain to be seen. At the other end of the fortress, on Piazza d'Armi, stands the small church, Nostra Signora di Regnos Altos, which was restored in 1975 to its original thirteenth-century appearance. The interior is richly frescoed by painters of the fourteenth-century Tuscan school. In the walls, behind the church, there is an unusual, octagonal bastion, built of grey, trachyte stone. It is possible to climb up onto the walls here and admire the splendid view of Bosa and the surrounding valley.

Leave Bosa by following Via Lungo Temo, along the river bank, towards the sea. After 3km (2 miles), there is a bridge leading to the modern resort of **Bosa Marina**. Situated at the mouth of the River Temo, the resort faces onto **Isola Rossa**, a pink, rocky islet. Formerly an island proper, it is now joined to the marina by a causeway. The fat watch-tower, surmounting the islet, was built by the Aragonese and dates from the seventeenth century.

The route forks right at the bridge, following the SS129bis which is signed to Alghero, before joining the SP49 Strada Panoramica. This narrow, but well-surfaced road follows the littoral, taking in some of the most beautiful coastal scenery in Sardinia. Boulders of pink rock reach out into the crystal waters, while the air is fragrant with the scent of *macchia* and wild rosemary.

The first landmark along the coast, is the abandoned watch-tower, **Torre Argentina**, which is 7km (4 miles) from Bosa. Those who wish to bathe, can make the 10-minute hike from here, towards the headland of **Capo Marargiu**, where there are several superb, deserted, sandy beaches. After passing the headland, the road crosses inland, affording excellent views of the sea in the distance. Continuing northwards, the road climbs along the base of Monte Mannu (802m/2,630ft), offering views of the pink-tinted cliffs that edge the vast bay ahead. The cliffs, which are made up of volcanic trachyte and tufa rock, are one of the last places of refuge of the Griffon Vulture. Other birds of prey, including the black vulture also nest on the crags. LIPU, the Sardinian bird protection society, have boosted the numbers of the black vulture, by importing and releasing birds here from Spain.

As the road dips up and down along the cliff tops, high above the sea, the scenery is outstanding. Dramatically coloured outcrops of rock, contrast with the verdant *macchia* and the crystal-blue sea. There are parking areas, at panoramic points along the road, from which to stop and enjoy the view. A few kilometres before reaching **Torre Poglina**, a ruined watch-tower which sits on a headland, there is a track on the left, leading to the beach, **Spiaggia Sa Mandra**. After passing the tower and the offshore islet, the road runs alongside the wide, sandy beach of **Poglina Spiaggia**, before climbing up once more into the hills. Vineyards and olive groves dot the landscape, and for the first time since leaving Bosa, there are signs of habitation. As the road rejoins the coast, 4km (2 ½ miles) south of Alghero, there are views of the blunt-ended headland, **Punta Giglio**, and the prominent, wedge-shaped cape, **Capo Caccia**, behind it. Tucked neatly into the bay, the road finally enters Alghero, which is the starting point of Route 6b.

Route 6B • Alghero and Environs

Route 6b enters **Alghero**, from the south, on Viale Kennedy. Follow the one-way system to Piazza Sulis, where there is a fee-paying carpark. Alternatively, look for a space on Lungomare Colombo, which leads from the north-west corner of Piazza Sulis, along the fortified sea walls. There is also another carpark at the northern end of the town, next to the port, but this involves tackling the one-way system and circumnavigating your way around the narrow streets in the historic centre, many of which are pedestrianised.

The historic centre of Alghero covers a small promontory which juts out into a wide, open bay. The promontory is defended on all sides by stout walls and bastions which were built by the Genoese in the eleventh century. The Genoans succeeded in transforming a sleepy fishing village into a well-defended and active trading centre, but the charm and character of Alghero today, is the legacy of Spanish rule. In 1353, the town was seized from the Genoans by Pedro IV of Aragon, and within 20 years the original population had been evicted, and people from Barcellona, Valencia and Mallorca re-settled in their place. The town's walls, which were largely rebuilt by the Spanish, then served not only to keep out marauding Arab invaders, but also any Sardinians who were not loyal to the regime. Only a limited number of Sardinian nationals were allowed residency, and at the sounding of a trumpet, any non-resident Sards had to evacuate the town. Life for the Spanish in Alghero was also strictly controlled, and residents were not allowed to travel more than a few kilometres away. Spanish domination ensued for four centuries and present-day Alghero is still more Spanish than Sardinian. The street names are written in Catalan and Italian: a *piazza* is a *placas*, a *via* (street) is a *carrer* and a *chiesa* (church) is an *iglesia*; and many of the locals still speak a Catalan dialect. The local cuisine is also Spanish-influenced, with dishes such as *paella* commonly seen on restaurant menus, and Catalan-style lobster a local speciality.

The singular character of Alghero has made it one of the most popular tourist destinations in Sardinia, particularly with the British. The cobbled streets are packed with restaurants, hotels and souvenir shops, and tourists literally rub shoulder to shoulder in peak season. However, the town is not only dependent on tourism, it also has a thriving fishing industry with the largest fishing port on the island. This lends the town genuine colour which together with the Catalan-Aragonese architecture make Alghero a fascinating place to visit.

Piazza Sulis, which is at the southern perimeter of the historic centre, is a good starting point for a tour of the town. On the western side of this piazza, there is a fat, round tower, Torre Sulis, which is named after Vincenzo Sulis who was imprisoned here for his involvement in the Cagliari riots against the Spanish in the eighteenth century. The tower has been standing, however, since the sixteenth century when it was built as one of the bastions in the fortified town wall. It is 23m (75ft) tall and has walls 5½m (18ft) thick, and contains large chambers on each of its two floors. From the tower, follow the sea walls along the promenade of Lungomare Colombo, where the piles of canon balls are a reminder of Alghero's troubled history. At the western end of Lungomare Colombo, some 250m (275yd) from Torre Sulis, is Torre Giacomo, a low, octagonal tower with crenellations, which was built in the fifteenth century. It is also known as the Torre deis Cutxos (Dog's Tower) as in the days of Spanish rule, stray dogs used to be locked up here. Opposite the tower, is the seventeenth-century church, Chiesa del Carmelo, which has a simple, stone façade. The interior holds its original Baroque pulpit and altar, both of which are carved from wood and decorated with gilt. Contained within the niches of the altar, from left to right, are statues of the Prophet Elias, the Madonna of Carmelo and St Teresa Davila respectively. Continue north of Torre Giacomo, along Lungomare Marco Polo. This pedestrianised street has tall, elegant houses with blue and green shutters and arched windows, which enjoy magnificent views across the bay of Alghero, to Capo Caccia. At the northern end of Lungomare Marco Polo, there is a lively port, filled with luxury yachts and fishing boats, but just before reaching it take the steps that lead up on the right, to the back of the Cattedrale.

Surrounded by a labyrinth of narrow streets and alleys, the Cattedrale was started in 1552, but was not completed until 1730, which was the year of its consecration. The apse, and the octagonal bell tower, which has an attractive roof of green and white tiles, are the oldest parts of the building and are typical of Catalan-Gothic

Pleasure yachts moored at Alghero marina

architecture of the sixteenth century. The portal is also a fine example of the Catalan-Gothic, although the rest of the façade is late Renaissance in style, with Doric columns arranged like a Classical temple portico. The octagonal dome is a late Renaissance addition too. The interior, which is divided into three tall naves, is furnished with marble altars and funerary monuments which date from the eighteenth century. Amongst the most important funerary monuments is that in the left transept, which belongs to Maurizio of Savoy, Duke of Monferrato, who was the brother of King Carlo Felice. It was commissioned by the King in 1807 and sculpted by Felice Festa. In the apse, there is a raised presbytery, at the back of which, there is an ambulatory with five radiating chapels. The chapels have their original Gothic vaults and arches.

From the Cattedrale façade, Via Erasmus runs directly due north. This street was once the centre of the Jewish quarter of Alghero. It is worth strolling along to see the ornately-decorated façade of Palau Reial which belonged to the Jewish Carcassona family until 1492. Return to the Cattedrale façade, and head east towards Porta Mare, one of the principal gates in the old town wall. It overlooks the busy fishing port where trawlers and fishing boats unload their daily haul. Just inside the gate, is Piazza Civica which is the town's main square. It is surrounded by Catalan-Aragonese Gothic *palazzi* which house smart cafés and souvenir shops. The grandest building on the *piazza* is Palazzo d'Albis, which dates from the sixteenth century, and was the residence of the local governors throughout the Spanish regime. The Spanish viceroys also resided here until they took up post in Cagliari. It is recorded that in 1541, Emperor Charles V stayed here on his way to Algiers and addressed the public from the balcony window.

From the western end of the *piazza*, take Via Carlo Alberto, which is the busiest street in the historic centre. Paved with dark flagstones, and lined with four-storey *palazzi* at either side, the street holds umpteen crafts and jewellery shops. Coral is one of Alghero's specialities and is very widely available. There are coral reefs off the coast to the north-west of the town, but not all the coral sold in Alghero is local. Some is imported, some is reconstituted, and some is plastic imitation from Taiwan. The price is a fair indication of what you are buying, and generally the most expensive items are fine works of local craftsmanship.

Continuing along Via Carlo Alberto, the church of San Francesco is passed on the left. Constructed with a coarse, creamy-coloured stone, the church dates from the second half of the fourteenth century, although alterations and additions were made in the sixteenth century. The architecture is therefore a blend of the Catalan-Aragonese Gothic and the Renaissance, a fact that is exemplified by the façade, the lower part of which is fourteenth century and the upper part sixteenth century. The interior of San Francesco is mainly of note for its Gothic presbytery which has a beautifully-decorated ceiling. The main altar, standing in the presbytery, is richly worked from coloured marbles and dates from the eighteenth century. The church was originally part of a Franciscan monastery, and the simple, but charming, cloisters have been well-restored. During the summer, they provide a delightful venue for a season of concerts.

A short distance further along Via Carlo Alberto, also on the left, there is another church, San Michele, which is easily distinguished by its bright-green, tiled dome. It was built in 1612 as part of a Jesuit college, and is sumptuously decorated inside with stucco altars and beautifully-carved and gilted, wooden choir stalls. Via Carlo Alberto finally ends at Piazza Sulis, the starting point of the tour, however, it is well worth spending some time wandering about the numerous back streets and cobbled alleys. One of the most interesting of the back streets is Via Principe Umberto, which at one time was the main artery through the town. It runs parallel with Via Carlo Alberto, and starts from the octagonal bell tower of the Cattedrale. Roughly midway along the street, is an elegant square, Piazza Vittorio Emanuele. It holds the excellently-restored Palazzo Machin which was the family home of Bishop Ambrogio Machin. Built in the early seventeenth century, it has a fine Renaissance portal and Catalan-Aragonese Gothic windows. To the north of the piazza, on the left, is Casa Doria, which dates from the sixteenth-century and has typical Catalan-Aragonese Gothic windows on each of the four storeys of its narrow façade.

Other features of interest in the town include Torre di Porta Terra which is on Piazza Porta Terra in the eastern town walls. Also known as Torre dels Hebreus, the tower was erected by the wealthy Jewish community of Alghero in the fifteenth century. It guarded the second of the town's principal gates, which were locked up every day at dusk, after the trumpet had sounded for non-residents to leave.

Back on Piazza Sulis, visit the Mare Nostrum Aquarium, which is just off the north-east corner of the square on Via XX Settembre. The aquarium has an impressive selection of fish and marine life found in the seas surrounding Sardinia, as well as in freshwater areas. There are about thirty well-kept tanks, the largest of which has typical species of the Mediterranean. Amongst the more unusual specimens in the aquarium are pirhanas, tropical sharks and alligator pikes.

A popular excursion by boat from Alghero is to the **Grotta di Nettuno**, which is on the tip of the headland, **Capo Caccia**. Boats depart regularly from the port, and tickets usually include entry to the grotto. The grotto can only be visited with a guide, who takes tours every hour. It is a very scenic trip, as the boat skirts around the base of the sheer, limestone cliffs before entering the cave mouth. The cave is rated amongst the most interesting in Sardinia due to the fact that it contains a large lake, Lago Marmora. The lake is inside the grotto's largest chamber, which is known as Sala della Reggia. There are fantastic stalactites and stalagmites and other concretions throughout the grotto, the best of which are illuminated.

It is also possible to visit the Grotta di Nettuno by road. To do so, follow signs out of Alghero to Fertilia. The road heads along the coast before joining a one-way system through the modern outskirts of the town where visitors may wish to stop by at the Museo Mineralogico, a museum of locally-found minerals. Just outside Alghero, a lagoon, **Stagno di Calich**, is passed on the right. The road crosses over the mouth of the lagoon, where there is a small fishing harbour and the remnants of a Roman bridge that was reconstructed in the medieval age. The town of **Fertilia**, which was built during Mussolini's campaign to develop rural Sardinia in 1936, is passed to the left. A

Anghelu Ruju *necropolis, hewn from rock and earth*

modern church spire marks the town centre, which is rather dull, having a uniform architecture and a rigid grid-plan street system.

The road continues past Fertilia, through neatly-ordered vineyards and pine forests. On the left, there is a small road to the beautiful, sandy beaches of **Le Bombarde** and **Lazzaretto**, which look across the bay to Alghero. A short distance further, on the right, approximately 10km (6 miles) from Alghero, is the ancient Nuraghic settlement of *Nuraghe Palmavera*. Constructed with great blocks of dazzling-white limestone, the ruins of this former village are centred around a well-preserved tower with a domed roof. Dating from 1100BC, some fifty circular huts have been excavated. Archaeological evidence indicates that the site was abandoned in the fifth century BC following a fire. The wealth of archaeological finds, that were uncovered during the excavations, are now in the Sassari museum.

A short distance beyond Nuraghe Palmavera, the road divides. The left fork leads to **Porto Conte**, a vast bay, which is enclosed by **Punta Giglio** in the east and **Capo Caccia** in the west. The route continues along the right fork, which follows the edge of the bay, although the water is screened from view by the rows of pines and eucalyptus trees that line the road. At the northern end of the bay, is the large holiday complex of **Baia de Grotte**, from where boats depart regularly for excursions, to Grotta di Nettuno amongst other destinations. There are also facilities for horse-riding and watersports here.

As the road proceeds around the bay, there are views across to **Torre Nuovo** on the opposite side. Another tower, **Torre Tramariglio**, is passed on the left and together with Torre Nuovo, guards the entrance to the bay. Beyond Torre Tramariglio, the great bulk of Capo Caccia looms ever nearer. The road finally ends, 25km (15 ½ miles) west of Alghero, at a carpark, from where the Grotta di Nettuno is reached by descending the Scala del Cabirol, an impressive flight of over 600 steps. It takes about 20 minutes to climb down and considerably longer to climb back up, but the scenery is good, as the steps scale the steep, white cliffs of the cape which overlooks the small offshore island, **Isola Foradada**. The cliffs around the cape are another place of refuge for the Griffon Vulture. LIPU (Italian League for the Protection of Birds) and WWF (World Wildlife Fund) ensure that the colony does not die out by depositing innards and carcasses at **Punta Cristallo**, which is on the western side of the cape.

Those who intend to continue onto Route 6c, do not need to return to Alghero, but can join the SS291 by following back along the bay of Porto Conte, as far as the Baia de Grotte holiday complex, shortly after which there is a turning on the left, signposted to Sassari.

Visitors should approach the SS291 crossroads, which is 14km (9 miles) to the north, with caution and take care to give way, as this junction is quite deceptive.

Route 6C • Alghero to Sassari

Travelling from Alghero on the SS291, which is signposted to Porto Torres, the first point of interest is the necropolis of *Anghelu Ruju*, which is on the left side of the road, immediately after the turning to Fertilia airport. The site entrance is easy to miss and is only indicated by a small, yellow sign. Proceed through the double gates at the roadside and follow the track for about 20m (22yd). It leads into a grassy field where the remains of the necropolis, dips and hollows in the red earth, is located. Excavators have dated the earliest parts of the necropolis to 3,000BC which is well before the era of the Nuraghic civilisation. This neolithic civilisation belonged to the Ozieri culture and were probably a simple fishing community. The burial chambers, of which thirty-eight have been recorded, are hewn from the rock and earth in a style which is referred to in other parts of Sardinia as *domus de janas* (witches' houses). Some have elliptical areas in front of their entrances which probably served as the place of cult worship or sacrifice. Cult figures, in the form of statuettes of female idols, suggesting that it might have been a matriarchal society, were found in the necropolis. They are on display in the archaeological museums in Sassari and in Cagliari.

Continuing along the SS291, in a northerly direction, wine-lovers should stop by at the Sella and Mosca Enoteca which is passed on the right. Set amongst immaculate vineyards, the Sella and Mosca estate is approached by a long, tree-lined, gravel drive. It is one of the largest wine estates in Europe and unlike most wine producers in Sardinia, it is not run as a co-operative, but is privately-owned. The selection of wines is wide-ranging, but perhaps the best souvenir is a bottle of Anghelu Ruju, which is named after the necropolis. It is made with the locally grown Cannonau grapes, which according to a traditional recipe, are semi-dried before being made into wine. The result is a rich and sweet, red dessert wine, the best of which, the *riserva*, has an alcohol content of up to 18 per cent. Sella and Mosca also produce one of Sardinia's best Vermentino, which is a light, white table wine, made with Vermentino grapes.

At the SS291 crossroads, visitors have the option of either turning right, and proceeding directly to Sassari, or keeping straight on to Porto Torres. **Porto Torres** is an unwieldy town with extensive industrial outskirts, oil refineries along its sea front, and a large port which deals with commerce as well as passenger ferries from mainland Italy and Corsica. However, it is also of historical interest, for it is the site of the first Roman city to have been built in Sardinia. Named *Turris Libyssonis*, the city was established in 27BC, and along with Cagliari in the south, was to become one of the most important harbours on the island. The most impressive Roman remains are to be found near the railway station. Known as the Palazzo di Re Barbaro, after the Roman Governor Barbarus, who resided here in the fourth century AD. The ruins are basically a baths complex, which dates from the city's foundation. Amongst the tumbled stones and columns, there are remnants of mosaic floors. Archaeological finds from the site are housed in the local Antiquarium.

The other major point of interest in Porto Torres, the church of San Gavino, is a monument to the Romanesque era, when the city was fought over by the Pisans and Genoese. The church stands nearby the Roman ruins, on a small hill at the west side of the town. It is the largest Romanesque church in Sardinia and was built in 1111 to house the relics of St Gavin, who was martyred here in AD300, when Barbarus was Governor. Now the town's patron saint, the relics of St Gavin still rest in the crypt, along with two other Christian martyrs.

An excursion can be made from Porto Torres, along the extreme north-western coast of Sardinia, to the small fishing village and resort of **Sintino** which is 29km (18 miles) away. It is built on a small promontory between two rocky harbours. There is an excellent sandy beach 2km (1 mile) further north, the **Spiaggia di Pelosa**, which runs along the tip of the headland, **Capo del Falcone**. Facing the beach is **Isola Piana** and the much larger island of **Isola Asinara**, which was where the present-day inhabitants of Stintino moved from in the nineteenth century. It is now a penal colony and visitors are not permitted onto the island. The waters around the headland, which are guarded by the well-preserved watch-tower, **Torre Pelosa**, are popular for sub-aqua diving and watersports facilities are available at Spiaggia di Pelosa which has become increasingly tourist-friendly over recent years.

From Porto Torres, head south-east on the SS131 to Sassari. This busy highway passes by an ancient place of sacrifice, known as **Monte d'Accodi**. It is to the right of the road, approximately 6km (4 miles) from Porto Torres. Dating from 2,000BC, it is a unique site, there being no other monument in Sardinia like it, although similar structures exist in Eastern Turkey and the Mesopotamian Plain. It consists of an earth mound, some 10m (33ft) high, which is surmounted by a platform with a megalithic sacrificial altar. It is believed that fertility rites were held here as well as sacrifices. There is also a burial area with tombs hewn from the rock, similar to the *domus de janas* (witches' houses) seen elsewhere in Sardinia.

Sassari, which is the starting point of Route 7a, lies a further 22km (14 miles) along the SS131. As the road approaches the city's outskirts, keep in lane, following the signs to *centro* and Viale Umberto, where parking spaces can be found.

A characteristically peaceful Sardinian scene

Additional Information

Places to Visit

Alghero
Cattedrale Santa Maria
Piazza Duomo
☎ 079 979222

Mare Nostrum Aquarium
Via XX Settembre 1
☎ 079 978333
Open: winter Saturday and Sunday
5-11pm. Summer daily 10am-1pm,
5-11pm.

Museo Mineralogico
Via Don Minzoni 159
☎ 079 953488
Open: Monday to Friday 6-8pm.

Bosa
Castello di Serravalle
(custodian)
Via Ultima Coasta 12
☎ 0785 33030
Open: winter daily 10am-1pm, 4-6pm.
Summer daily 10am-1pm, 4-7pm.

Capo Caccia
Grotta di Nettuno
☎ 079 946540
Visit by guided tour only
Open: winter daily 9am-3pm, guided
tour every hour, last tour 2pm. Summer daily 8am-8pm, guided tour
every hour, last tour 7pm.

Porto Torres
Museo Antiquario
Via Ponte Romano
☎ 079 514433
Open: Tuesday to Satursay 9-1.30pm.
Sunday 9-1pm.

Useful Information

Alghero
Sports Facilities
Corallo Sub (Diving Centre)
Via Matteotti 61
☎ 079 977519

International Diving Centre
Via Garibaldi 13
☎ 079 952433

Poseidon Club (Diving Centre)
Via G. Ferret 11
☎ 079 978407

Cooperativa Hermeu
(Windsurf and Sailing)
Spiaggia Maria Pia
☎ 079 951976

North West Windsurfing
Spiaggia Le Bombarde
☎ 079 976470

Stabilimento Balneare Novelli
(Windsurf and Sailing)
Via Lido 18
☎ 079 950343

Yacht Club Alghero
Banchino Porto
☎ 079 952074

Campo Tennis (Tennis)
Regina Maria Pia
☎ 079 953083

Campo Tennis (Tennis)
Via Tarragona
☎ 079 979915

Club Ippico Capuano
(Horse Riding Centre)
Strada Alghero-Villanova
☎ 079 978198

Tourist Information Centre
Azienda Autonoma di Soggiorno e
    Turismo
Piazza Porta Terra 9
☎ 079 979262

Transport
Aeroporto Civile (Airport)
Fertilia
☎ 079 935043

Ati Scalo Aeroporto (Airport)
Fertilia ☎ 079 935033

Stazione Ferroviaria (Railway)
Via Don Minzoni ☎ 079 950785

ARST (Bus)
Stazione Autobus
Via Catalogna ☎ 079 260048

Avis (Car Hire)
Piazza Sulis 9 ☎ 079 979577

Avis (Car Hire)
Aeroporto Fertilia ☎ 079 935064

Hertz (Car Hire)
Aeroporto Fertilia ☎ 079 935054

Maggiore (Car Hire)
Piazza Sulis 1
☎ 079 979375

Maggiore (Car Hire)
Aeroporto Fertilia ☎ 079 935045

Cunedda Viaggi (Bicycle and
    Motorbike Hire)
Via La Marmora 34
☎ 079 952386

Velosport (Bicycle and Motorbike
    Hire)
Via Vittorio Veneto 90
☎ 079 977182

Alice Nautica (Boat Hire)
Porta a Mare 2
☎ 079 980370

Catalan Boat (Boat Hire)
Spiaggia del Calik
☎ 079 978620

Nanoya Charter (Boat Hire)
Via Carlo Alberto 109
☎ 079 978868

Compagnia Navisarda (Ferry)
Porto
☎ 079 975599

Societa Punta del Dentul (Ferry)
Cala Dragonara ☎ 079 946642

Travel Agencies
Agenzie Marittime Sarde
Via Vittorio Emanuele 27
☎ 079 979005

Agritours
Via Ugo Foscolo 10 ☎ 079 974329

Magic Tours
Piazza Sulis 11 ☎ 079 979539

Parodo Tours
Piazza Sulis 15 ☎ 079 979577

Emergencies
Polizia Urbana (Town Police)
Via Brigata Sassari 7
☎ 079 997800

Carabinieri (Military Police)
Via Simon 5
☎ 079 979038

Assistenza Medica per Turisti
(Medical Service for Tourists)
Via Pola
Fertilia ☎ 079 930396
Open: 1 July to 10 September.

Guardia Medica (Medical Officer)
Ospedale Traumatologico
☎ 079 950613

Pronto Soccorso (First Aid Service)
Ospedale Civile
Via Don Minzoni ☎ 079 951096

Servizio Ambulanza (Ambulance
    Service)
Misericordia Alghero
Via Giovanni XXIII 64
☎ 079 976634

Automobile Club d'Italia
Via Mazzini 56
☎ 079 979659

Bosa
Events and Festivals
17 January, Festa di Sant'Antonio. (Festival of St Anthony and first day of the carnival 'Carnevale Bosano').

24-25 April, Festa di San Giorgio. (Cultural events celebrating festival of San Giorgio).

28 May, Festa dei Santi Emilio e Priamo. (Folk and musical events celebrating the patron saints of the town, Santi Emilio e Priamo).

24 June, Festa di San Giovanni Battista. (Horse race and poetry competition).

29 June, Festa dei Santi Pietro e Paolo. (Festival of St Peter and Paul celebrated with a regatta and a fair of local products).

First Sunday August, Festa di Santa Maria del Mare. (Festival of Santa Maria del Mare, procession by boat from Bosa Marina to Bosa with sacred image of the Madonna. Festival ends with entertainments and firework display).

Second Sunday September, Sagra di Nostra Signora di Regnos Altos. (Procession, gastronomy stands, Sardinian song and dance competition).

Sports Facilities
Scuola Surf
Bosa Marina
☎ 0785 373400

Equitazione (Horse Riding)
Strada Bosa Marina
☎ 0785 373092

Canottaggio (Canoeing)
Via Roma
☎ 0785 373329

Tourist Information Centres
Pro Loco
Via Ciusa
☎ 0785 373580

Comune
Piazza Carmine
☎ 0785 373114

Transport
Trasporti per Mare Avellino Porto Turistico (Boat)
☎ 0785 373617

Travel Agencies
Agenzia Viaggi
Corso Vittorio Emanuele
☎ 0785 374391

Emergencies
Carabinieri (Military Police)
Piazza Carmine
☎ 0785 373116

Ospedale (Hospital)
Via Salvatore Parpaglia
☎ 0785 373107

Croce Rossa (Ambulance)
Viale Italia
☎ 0785 373818

Guardia Medica Turistica (Medical Officer)
Viale Italia ☎ 0785 374615

Automobile Club d'Italia
Via Giovanni XXIII 31
☎ 0785 374259

Stintino
Tourist Information Centre
Azienda Autonoma di Soggiorno e Turismo
Via Colombo 80
☎ 079 523160

7

SASSARI AND THE NORTH-WEST

Chapter 7 explores the fascinating city of Sassari and the province of the same name. Sassari is the smartest city on the island and offers the visitor many attractions. The surrounding province, known in medieval times as Logudoro, 'Land of Gold', is also full of interest. The route passes through the heart of Logudoro, where the now-sleepy town of Ardara was once capital. The Logudoro has some twenty or more Romanesque churches, dotted about the countryside, as testimony to the region's wealth and importance in medieval times, most of which were commissioned by trading merchants, and designed by architects from Tuscany. The route takes in a good number of these churches, all of which are easily accessible. Unfortunately, few are open to the public, but the architectural quality of their exteriors, and the beauty of their locations, means that they are nonetheless worth visiting.

Another important feature of the region, are the great number of Nuraghic settlements. The greatest concentration of settlements is to be found approximately 40km (25 miles) south of Sassari in an area now called the Valle dei Nuraghe. Chapter 7 takes in the most impressive of the Nuraghic settlements here, namely *Santu Antine*.

The cuisine of Sassari and its province, is typical of the Sardinian interior, with most dishes based on lamb or pork. Offal is quite widely eaten too, as are snails (*lumache*.) Perhaps more enticing is the selection of pastries available. *Sebadas*, pastries filled with soft white cheese and served with honey or sugar, are particularly worth looking out for. An excellent accompaniment to pastries such as these, is the rich fortified Moscato wine, that is produced to the north of Sassari.

The route is divided into four sections each of which can be covered in a day or two. The last section of the route, Route 7d, can be missed for those that wish to make a round trip back to Sassari. Route 7d is also the most tortuous section of the itinerary in terms of driving and extra time should be allowed for the winding roads and hilly terrain.

Route 7A • Sassari

Sassari is undoubtedly the finest city in Sardinia, even though it is   ✳ second in size to Cagliari, the capital. It has a well-reputed university, a good basketball team and an important petro-chemicals industry. The standard of living here is higher than anywhere else on the island, and the central shopping streets are lined with very chic boutiques and smart cafés. At the same time, there are medieval back streets where life goes on in an old-fashioned way, and a lively district of cheap restaurants and *pizzerie*. It is definitely a young person's city, and because of its affluence sees little of the crime that plagues so many of Italy's southern cities.

Sassari first rose to importance in the medieval era with the debacle in fortune of the formerly superior city, Porto Torres, whose inhabitants were forced to flee inland from seaborne invaders. At this time, the wealthy, Genoan merchant family, the Dorias, made Sassari their capital and brought great prosperity to the city. The city continued to flourish as a trading centre under the Aragonese, and was to develop as a nucleus of intellectual and cultural progress. In 1617, the first university in Sardinia was established by the Jesuit community, since when, any number of notable figures have emerged from the city, including politicians such as the ex-president, Francesco Cossiga, and the leader of the former Italian Communist Party, the late Enrico Berlinguer.

A good starting point for a tour of the city, is the **Museo Nazionale**   🏛 **G.A. Sanna**, which is to the south of the historic centre, on Via Roma. The museum is composed of a gallery, an archaeological section and an ethnographical section, all of which are well-endowed. The collection was founded sixty years ago by Giovanni Antonio Sanna, but since then, Sassari University has donated archaeological finds, and other donations have been made by private collectors. The exhibits are arranged around eighteen well-organised rooms.

The first room in the archaeological section documents the earliest civilisation, neolithic man, in Sardinia. In the following room, there are finds from the sacrificial altar of Monte d'Acoddi (see Route 6c), including ceramics, idols, utensils and tools. The next two rooms hold finds from the early civilisations of Ozieri and Bonu Ighinu, which were found in a cave in the Mara region. There are also ceramics which are ascribed to another early culture, known as Monte Claro. Room F has material from the early Bronze Age, which has been excavated from necropoli all over Sardinia, such as bell-shape vases, decorated ceramics, figurines and also a number of skulls that were found between Sassari and Alghero.

On the first floor there is an excellent collection of Nuraghic finds, including plates, pans, jugs, cooking vessels with tripods, and jars which were found complete with bronze utensils inside. There are also ingots of copper ready to be forged. The collection of bronze figurines are ascribed to the late Nuraghic period and represent warriors, women, animals, boats, Nuraghic forts and deer. There is also an interesting display showing the development of Nuraghic architecture, which is illustrated with scale models. The other rooms on this floor contain archaeological material dating from the Phoenician and Carthaginian periods, including stelae from the necropolis of *Sulcis*, through to Roman, Byzantine and medieval times. Amongst the Roman exhibits are oil lamps, glass, ceramics, sarcophagi, and mosaics. There is also a coin collection which dates from the Punic era, up until the Savoy period of the nineteenth century.

The ethnographical section has a good collection of folkloric material from various regions in Sardinia, and includes textiles, lace, ceramics, work tools and household items. In the gallery there is a collection of some fifty paintings, which are arranged in chronological order, from the fourteenth century up to the nineteenth century. Of particular note are the Pisan triptych of *Saints Nicholas, Anthony and Laurence*, and the *Madonna with Child* by B. Vivarini, which dates from 1473.

From the museum, turn right and follow Via Roma, passing the severe, pink-stone façade of the *tribunale* (law courts) on the left. Approximately 400m (437yd) from the museum, Via Roma leads into the city's most impressive square, **Piazza d'Italia**, which covers an area of 1 hectare (2 acres), and was constructed in 1872. Along the north-east side, is the **Palazzo del Governo**, which was built between 1873 and 1880. It has a grand, neo-Classical façade with Corinthian columns and a rusticated base, and is surmounted by a translucent clock face. On the opposite side of the piazza, is the neo-Gothic **Palazzo Giordano**, which was built in 1878 and is now the seat of the Banca di Napoli. A monumental statue of King Vittorio Emanuele II commands the centre of the piazza, along with four graceful palm trees. The statue dates from 1889 and is a favourite perch for the mass of local pigeons. Around sunset, the piazza fills with all the young people of the city, on their mopeds or arm-in-arm, catching up on the latest gossip. The great sea of voices in the evening air is a memorable experience.

From Piazza Italia, follow the arcaded street, that leads from the north-western side of the square, into **Piazza Castello**. Named after the Aragonese castle that stood here until 1877, when it was pulled down, this long and thin piazza is now surrounded by high-rise apartments, and is something of a race track for the local traffic, which tears around its palm-lined centre. Continue through Piazza Castello, to **Corso Vittorio Emanuele**, which leaves from the northern end of the square. This narrow, cobbled, shopping street is the main artery through the historic centre of Sassari. It slopes downhill, finishing at Piazza Sant'Antonio, which is near the railway station, and becomes more run-down the further you progress along it. Most of Sassari's cheap restaurants are centred around here either in the numerous alleys that branch off either side, or along the Corso itself.

Roughly midway along Corso Vittorio Emanuele, the theatre, which was erected in 1830, is passed on the right. At this point, take the left turn along Via del Duomo for 150m (164yd) to the duomo. Built of white limestone, the **duomo** dates from the thirteenth century, although what is seen today is mostly seventeenth century. Only the multi-sided *campanile*, which stands at the back of the church, on the left, remains of the original structure. The decorative style of the building is typical of the Spanish Baroque, with the addition of that distinctive Sardinian touch. The façade has three spacious arches along its base, supporting a rusticated upper section, which is pierced by three elaborately-carved niches with statues and medallions. The uppermost section of the façade, shaped like Nelson's hat, is the most fancifully decorated, with a profusion of carved, curling foliage surrounding the papal statue that is seated in the central niche.

It is worth spending some time exploring the narrow, twisting streets that surround the duomo, taking in some of the sixteenth-century, Gothic-Catalan architecture that characterises the historic centre. **Via Turitana**, which leads from the back right side of the duomo, is one of the many attractive, flag-stoned streets, with small shops selling local produce, jewellers' workshops, and a number of simple restaurants. On a piazza to the south of Via Turritana, is the university with its severe neo-Classical façade. The back of the **university** looks onto the **public gardens**, where there are many big, shady trees. As well as greenery, there is also a children's playground, and a fountain which has a life-size statue of St Francis leaning on one side, talking to the birds that are perched on the rim. At the southern end of the gardens, there is an exhibition room,

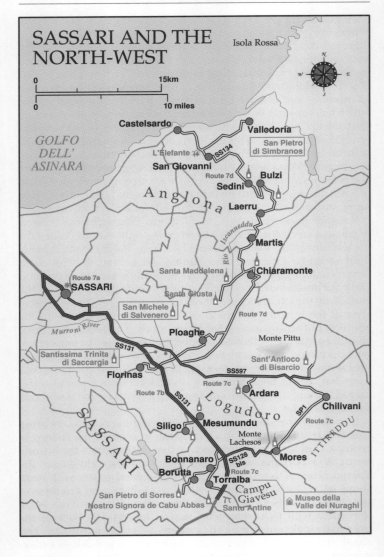

SASSARI AND THE NORTH-WEST

Isola Rossa

| 0 | 15km |
| 0 | 10 miles |

Castelsardo

Valledoria

GOLFO DELL' ASINARA

San Pietro di Simbranos

L'Elefante

SS134

San Giovanni

Route 7d

Bulzi

Sedini

Laerru

Anglona

Martis

Rio Iscanneddu

Santa Maddalena

Chiaramonte

Santa Giusta

Route 7d

San Michele di Salvenero

Route 7a

SASSARI

Ploaghe

Monte Pittu

Murroni River

SS131

Santissima Trinita di Saccargia

Sant'Antioco di Bisarcio

Florinas

SS597

Route 7c

Route 7b

SS131

Logudoro

Ardara

SP1

Chilivani

Route 7c

Siligo

Mesumundu

Monte Lachesos

Mores

ITTIREDDU

SASSARI

Bonnanaro

SS128 bis

Borutta

Route 7c

Torralba

San Pietro di Sorres

Nostra Signora de Cabu Abbas

Campu Giavesu

Santu Antine

Museo della Valle dei Nuraghi

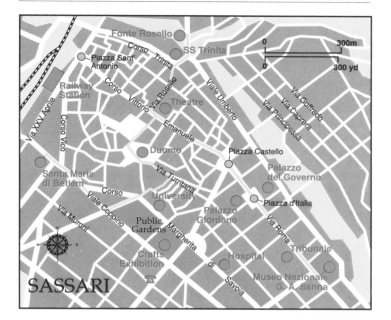

which holds a permanent display of Sardinian crafts, including textiles, baskets, leather, pottery, wood carvings and jewellery. It is possible to purchase many of the objects on display, which is well worth doing, as the quality of the workmanship is good and the prices reasonable.

Other points of interest in Sassari include the church of **Santa Maria di Betlem**, which can be reached by taking Viale Coppino from the northern end of the gardens. Situated on the left side of the street, it has its original thirteenth-century, Romanesque façade which is pierced by a fine portal and rose window. The interior has Gothic vaults, a feature that was added in the fifteenth century, and richly-carved altars, dating from the eighteenth century, along either side of the central aisle. To the left of the eliptical-shaped cupola, there is a wood-carved statue of the *Madonna and Child* which dates from the fourteenth century. It is in the cloisters of this church that the *candelieri*, 3m (10ft)-high candle holders, are stowed away. The *candelieri* are brought out once a year, along with banners and other medieval paraphernalia, for the fantastic procession that takes place in Sassari on 14 August (see Additional Information at the end of this chapter).

Those prepared to wander off the beaten track, may wish to visit the Renaissance fountain which is just outside the medieval city walls, on the north-eastern side of the city. To get there, return to Corso Vittorio Emanuele, and take Via Rosello, which branches off near the theatre. The street ends on Corso Trinita, opposite the church of SS Trinita, from where steps lead down to **Fonte Rosello**. The fountain was built in 1605, over a natural spring which provided the city with drinking water. It is attractively carved, with statues representing the seasons at each of its four corners and an equestrian statue of St Gavin on top.

Route 7B • Sassari to Santu Antine

Leave Sassari, either by taking the ring road which is signed to Cagliari, or by taking the road to Olbia, which zig-zags down the steep, limestone table mountain on which the city stands. Once out of the city, the visitor should follow the SS131, in the direction of Cagliari. This busy dual-carriageway carves through the hills, following the Murroni river valley. The road leaves the valley at the Ploaghe junction, but visitors should continue on the SS131, through the Logudoro hills, to Florinas. The flat-topped hills are given over to sheep grazing and the landscape is criss-crossed with dry-stone walls. Logudoro, which once encompassed the entire north-western corner of the island, was one of the four judiciaries that controlled Sardinia in medieval times.

Continuing for 11km (7 miles) from the Ploaghe junction, the road passes by **Siligo**, a small village, nearby which, there is a thirteenth-century church, called the Basilica del Signor del Regno. Shortly after the village, another church, known as Mesumundu, is passed to the left of the road. It stands in ruins, but has an attractive rustic simplicity. As the road continues southwards, the amount of land covered by vineyards increases, and at **Bonnanaro**, which is where visitors should turn off the SS131, there is a *cantina* (wine shop) which sells the local Montesanto wine to the public. Fork right at the outskirts of Bonnanaro, and head along the high street, which is lined with attractive, painted houses.

From Bonnanaro, a scenic country road leads gently up along a ridge, which overlooks the village of Torralba in the valley below. The road continues through **Borutta**, where an eleventh-century chapel, Santa Croce, is passed on the right. Follow signs from Borutta, to the Basilica di San Pietro di Sorres. At the second hairpin bend, above Borutta, turn off left.

The church and adjoined monastery of **San Pietro di Sorres** lie straight ahead, on a spur of land, which overlooks both Bonnanaro and Borutta. On top of the spur are a series of gently rolling fields, neatly edged with stone walls. In stark contrast to this pastoral setting, the façade of San Pietro di Sorres has a technical precision that recalls the city architecture of Florence or Pisa. It is decorated with bands of black and white stone, and sharply-delineated, geometric designs in coloured stones. It was once a cathedral, belonging to and founded by the Cistercians, an order that originated from the Cisteaux monastery in France. It was built for them in the twelfth century by Pisan architects, although the richness of its decor also suggests something of a French influence.

Five blind arcades span the lower part of the façade, with seven much smaller arcades and a mullioned window above. The topmost section, which is unusually high, holds a further three blind arcades and is distinctively striped in black and white. Each of the blind arcades contains a small, diamond-shaped window which is offset against a black and white geometric surround. In the spandrels of each arcade there is minute chequerboard patterning. The overall effect is striking.

The interior, since its restoration, is also impressive. The central nave is lined along either side with square pillars, which support black and white striped arches. The main apse is similarly decorated with bold stripes, while the ceiling has cross vaults of black basalt which are picked out with white. To the left of the main door, is a simply-carved, open sarcophagus, which once contained the mortal remains of Goffredo Benedetto, who was bishop from 1143 to 1153. On the ledge above the sarcophagus there is a statue of a Cistercian monk. Other features of interest in the church include the pulpit, which stands to the right of the raised presbytery. It is supported by four Gothic arches and has intricately inlaid medallions on each of its four sides. Suspended in the apse, there is the original, wooden-painted crucifix, although the altar is a modern addition.

From San Pietro di Sorres, return back through Borutta and Bonnanaro. At the bottom of the hill, below Bonnanaro, turn right and follow the valley to Torralba, which is 2km (1 mile) away. There are good views of San Pietro di Sorres, perched on its high bluff, and also of Borutta. **Torralba** is located on a small hill, and is mainly of interest for its museum, which houses remains from the nearby Nuraghic site of *Santu Antine*. The museum is on the left, just before the central square. Opened in 1988, the museum contains a modest but well-displayed and informative collection. On the ground floor there is an ethnographical collection which is mainly comprised of folk costumes, many of which derive from the old Logudoro region.

The statue of King Vittorio Emanuele II commands the centre of Piazza d'Italia, Sassari

The decorative stone masonry of Sassari cathedral

Sassari's public gardens

The ground floor also has a scale model of *Santu Antine* in the Sala Plastico. On the first floor, the main room, Sala Santu Antine, holds pottery fragments and other relics which were uncovered during the excavation of the site. The finds date from the tenth century BC. The other two rooms on the first floor have photographs of local Nuraghic settlements, of which there are a great many, thus giving the valley its name, the 'Valle dei Nuraghi'. Leave the museum by passing through a small garden, where there is a collection of *cippi* (tomb stones), dating from the Roman era.

Follow the high street through Torralba, and continue south-west on a minor road which runs parallel with the SS131. After a short distance, the road forks left and the Nuraghic site of *Santu Antine* is seen on the right. The ruins, along with *Barumini*, are the best-preserved and most extensive of their kind in Sardinia. They are strikingly situated on the Campu Giavesu plain where the horizon is only broken by the flat-topped hills of Logudoro. The megalithic stones of black basalt, which are used in the construction of the fort, are highlighted with a vivid-orange lichen that has grown over the centuries, and are in strong contrast to the occasional block of white limestone. Ringed by a finely-built wall of basalt, the site is approached by a track from a small carpark near the custodian's house.

At the core of this Nuraghic complex, is a gigantic tower, dating from the fourteenth century BC, which is 17 ½m (57ft) tall and is 15 ½m (51ft) in diameter. The three other towers, which are interconnected by a surrounding wall and form a triangular-shaped bastion, were added in the eighth century BC. The gateway through the bastion, leads past a guard room, which has two arrow slits, into an inner courtyard. There are no less than six entrances leading from the courtyard, the central one of which leads into the main tower. To explore the interior either take a torch, or hire one of the lamps that are available at the tower entrance. On the ground floor, there are three small chambers which are connected by a passage. To the left of the entrance a ramp spirals its way up between the massive walls, which are up to 5m (16ft) thick, to the first floor. Here, there is one large, circular room, covered by a domed, stone ceiling. It has a south-facing window, which looks onto a reconstructed Nuraghic tower in the field beyond. For much better views, continue up to the roof terrace. Back down in the courtyard, the two doors at the extremities lead into two of the towers that are part of the bastion, while the other doorways lead into a gallery. The gallery runs inside the bastion walls and is pierced by well-preserved, slit windows.

Other ruins surround the fortress, including the remains of Roman housing on the north-east side. From the northern side of the fortress, which is reached by following the footpath along the base of its walls, there are views across the plain to the ruined church, **Nostra Signora de Cabu Abbas**. Built atop a small plateau, only the apse remains of this Romanesque church with its distinctive black and white striped masonry.

Route 7C • Santu Antine to Ploaghe

From *Santu Antine*, return to the SS131, and head back, in the direction of Sassari for 6km (4 miles), to the junction with the SS128bis. Turn right at the junction, and follow the SS128bis to the town of **Mores**, which is 5km (3 miles) away. The parish church in Mores, Santa Caterina, has an unusually tall *campanile*. It is six storeys high, with columns decorating each level, and a statue of the Madonna at the very top. The church has a simple, but neatly-kept interior, with a single aisle and three chapels along either side. The ceilings of the chapels have their original, stone, barrel-vaults, although the main body of the church is plastered.

Continue downhill through Mores, following signs to Olbia and Chilivani. Just outside the town, the road passes by the dramatically-eroded ridge of Monte Lachesos (546m/1,791ft), to the left. After 3km (2 miles), visitors should fork left on the SP1, which is signposted to Olbia. The road crosses the Campu Giavesu plain, which is dotted with cork trees, passing by the jagged ridge of the Ittireddu outcrop, to the right. **Chilivani**, which is 10km (6 miles) north of the junction, is renowned for its racecourse and has extensive horse-breeding stables. The town also has a reputation for a local delicacy, almond cakes called *suspiros*.

After Chilivani, fork left for 5km (3 miles), before reaching the SS597, where visitors should turn right. Follow the SS597, until reaching the left turn, which is signposted to the SS132Marcus. The road leads up to the foot of a hillock, atop which are the derelict remains of **Sant'Antioco di Bisarcio**. Visitors should park next to the yellow-painted farm buildings on the left and then proceed on foot. Take the footpath from the back left corner of the farm, and continue up the steps that eventually lead to the church façade. The church, which is in a sorry state of repair, is built of a soft, pinkish stone and stands on natural rock foundations of the same colour.

It was first built in 1090, although it was entirely reconstructed less than a century later, when it became one of the principal cathedrals in the Logudoro, and was the setting for the coronations of several of the local *giudici*. Unlike other Romanesque churches in the region, the façade is preceded by a graceful portico, which has twin arches

The unusually tall bell tower of Santa Caterina Church, Mores

Sant' Antioco di Bisarcio Church, showing detail of the façade

The striking black and white façade of Santissima Trinita di Saccargia cloisters

at either side and a stone vaulted ceiling. The interior is not open to the public, but it is worth walking round to the back of the church to admire its fine apse. It is pierced by a series of diamond-shaped windows, which are framed by elegant blind-arcading. The square bell tower also stands at the back of the church, although sadly, the upper part has tumbled to the ground.

From Sant'Antioco di Bisarcio, return to the SS597, and turn right, in the direction of Sassari. The road follows a broad valley, which is dotted with cork trees, for 7km (4 miles), before reaching a turning on the left to **Ardara**. This small village lies on a low hilltop, 3km (2 miles) from the main road, and is mainly of interest for the recently-restored church, Santa Maria del Regno. Built in typical Romanesque style, the church dates from the twelfth century. After becoming a cathedral in 1239, it was the venue for the marriage of Enzo, son of the Hohenstaufen Emperor Frederick II, and Adelaida. Adelaida's dowry included the judiciaries of Torres and Gallura, which when put together with Logudoro, formed a sizeable part of the island. This led Enzo to proclaim himself King of Sardinia, although he spent little time either in Ardara, which was then the capital of Logudoro, or anywhere else on the island. Should you be fortunate enough to find the interior of Santa Maria del Regno open, do not miss the impressive, sixteenth-century tableau which is made up of 30 panels on a gold ground.

From Ardara, return to the SS597, and continue westwards, for a further 10km (6 miles), to the Ploaghe-Florinas junction. The countryside here is gently undulating, with dark, basalt stone walls edging the fields and vineyards. The only blot on the landscape, is the power station at the Ploaghe-Florinas junction, which is passed to the left of the road, just before the charming Romanesque church of **Sant'Antonio**. To reach Sant'Antonio follow the track, which is signposted on the left, and proceed on foot through the rusty gate. The church stands on a rise, in the middle of a lush, green field. It is built of a motley collection of stones, including dark basalt, red travertine and white limestone, all of which are slightly irregularly shaped. This, combined with its squat dimensions, lend the church a rustic character. The central section is striped with coarse bands of red and white stone and has a simple decorative edge along the tops of the walls. The effect is perhaps most impressive at the back of the church, where the rounded apse is also banded in red and white.

From Sant'Antonio, it is a stone's throw to the next Romanesque church on the itinerary. **San Michele di Salvenero**, as it is named, is located on the left of the SS597. Be warned, however, that the turning to the church is very abrupt, and caution should be taking crossing over the heavy, oncoming traffic. The church was built in the twelfth century, and is typical of the Romanesque style of the era, with just a hint of French architecture about it. It is constructed of recently-cleaned, white stone, and has a tall central section which is flanked at either side by pilasters. It has odd transepts, that on the left being decorated with bands of black and white stone, while that on the right is plain and much smaller in size. It also has a fine triple apse, reminiscent of French architecture of the era, which is decorated with slender, blind arcades and a truncated *campanile*.

Undoubtedly the most impressive of the Romanesque churches in this region, is that of **Santissima Trinita di Saccargia**, which lies 3km (2 miles) beyond San Michele di Salvenero, on the SS597. The road dips down into a broad valley, which is cultivated with almond orchards and vineyards. The church, which is on the left, cannot be missed with its striking black and white striped *campanile* that dominates the landscape for miles around. Park at the pull-in, indicated on the left, and head on foot to the façade of this grand edifice.

It was originally built in 1116, although the striking, black and white striped façade was not added until just over a half-century later. The foundations were laid by the *giudice* of Logudoro in thanks to the Virgin Mary for his wife's fertility. It was the Pisans, however, who embellished the structure with its fancy masonry, including the intricately-inlaid medallions that decorate the upper façade. Pisan architects were also responsible for the addition of the portal, which is arcaded on all sides, with its arches resting on finely-carved capitals, that depict mythical, winged beasts. Carvings of animals also decorate the main door in a frieze of snarling beasts and rich foliage. The apse of the church is the oldest remaining part of the original structure and can be clearly distinguished by the coarseness of the stonework. The interior is rarely to be found open, however, the decor is quite plain, apart from a cycle of thirteenth-century frescoes, which are in need of restoration. Wandering around the exterior of the church the visitor will notice the ruins of the former-abbey buildings, including a row of arches that are the remains of its cloisters.

From Santissima Trinita di Saccargia, visitors have the option either to return to Sassari, which is 15km (9 miles) further along the SS597, or to continue on Route 7d which starts at Ploaghe. To reach Ploaghe return back along the SS597, forking left at the Ploaghe-Florinas junction, and then right. Ploaghe is just over 2km (1 mile) from the junction.

Route 7D • Ploaghe to Castelsardo

The small town of **Ploaghe** stands on a hill in the heart of the Logudoro countryside. The main road through the town centre, Corso G. Spano, leads to the façade of the parish church, San Pietro. Rather confusingly, there are in fact two churches here, side by side. That on the right is the older of the two and houses a small collection of paintings which can be seen by applying to the parish priest. It includes works by artists of the Tuscan, Flemish, Spanish and Sardinian schools. The much larger church, on the left, has a neo-Classical façade, with a broken pediment above the central door, and a pair of clock faces in the upper walls. The interior is quite plain with a single nave and chapels along either side. The first door on the left, leads into an adjoining cemetery, which has a number of old tombstones with Sardinian inscriptions. Before leaving Ploaghe, do not miss the fine views from the panoramic terrace, to the far right of San Pietro. The terrace looks out, across gentle valleys and hills, to the peak of Monte Pittu which is 488m (1,600ft) above sea level.

A narrow road, to the left of San Pietro, leads out of Ploaghe and crosses a rural landscape, which is dotted with small hillocks and flat-topped hills, before re-joining the main road. Heading in the direction of Tempio, the road slopes gently down, for 6km (4 miles), to a junction, at which point visitors should turn left to **Chiaramonte**. This small village is scenically-positioned on a summit, 430m (1,410ft) above sea level. Perched on a spur, that overhangs a rolling panorama, is the parish church with its belfry of dark, basalt stone. Above it, at the highest point of the town, is a ruined tower, which overlooks the countryside for many miles around. The road continues through Chiaramonte, and then winds down into the Rio Iscanneddu valley, where there are two rather remote churches, Santa Maddalena and Santa Giusta. Both are reached by a track which is signposted on the left, and lie at distances of 2km (1 mile) and 4km (2 miles) respectively, from the road.

The route continues through the agricultural village of **Martis**, which is surrounded by olive groves and vineyards. Beyond Martis, there are fine views, to the right of the road, across the treeless lowlands, which form part of the district of Anglona. The road proceeds, winding up and down, through this open landscape, where limestone boulders crest bare hillocks, until reaching another agricultural village, **Laerru**, which is also surrounded by olive groves and vineyards. At Laerru, visitors may wish to make the short diversion to the panoramic spot of Belvedere Fonte Concula, which is signposted at the village outskirts on the left. The main road,

One of Sardinia's most popular natural monuments is L'Elefante (Elephant Rock)

however, continues to wind through the village, passing the central piazza, where there is a memorial, before heading down to a junction. At the junction, visitors should turn left onto the SS134, which is signposted to Castelsardo.

The road winds through the bare, stony hills to the Romanesque church of **San Pietro di Simbranos**. The church is located below the road, on the right, and is accessible by an unsignposted track. Built in the twelfth century, this neatly-designed edifice has an attractive, striped façade of pink, black and white stone. The lower walls of the façade have blind arcades, in the typical Romanesque style, with a portal at the centre, while the upper walls are topped by a pediment. The interior, which is unfortunately rarely to be found open, holds a significant thirteenth-century, sculpted crucifixion, made of wood.

The road continues past San Pietro di Simbranos, and gradually climbs up to **Bulzi**, which has little to offer the visitor apart from an attractive, spired church. From Bulzi, the road winds up further still to the charming village of **Sedini**, which lies at a height of 300m (984ft). Many of Sedini's buildings date from the Aragonese period, and the most notable monument of this era is the church of Sant'Andrea. To reach the church, take the first turning on the right, and then turn right again, along a narrow alleyway which leads into a piazza. The piazza, which is surrounded by colourfully-painted *palazzi*, holds the church in one corner. Built in 1517, the church is typical of the Gothic-Aragonese style that spread throughout Sardinia in the sixteenth century. The square portal is carved in the traditional manner, as are the ogee-arched windows, which pierce the façade above. To the left of the façade there is a fine *campanile* which is surmounted by a pointed, stone top. The interior of the church is comprised of a single nave, which terminates in a wide apse, recessed inside a pointed arch. The chapels along either side of the nave, are also contained within pointed arches. The arches, which are decorated with a twisted design, rest on naively-carved capitals that depict figures and flying angels, intertwined with foliage. Pointed arches also decorate the inner wall of the entrance, where there is an attractive balcony.

On the way out of Sedini, the road passes a small complex of rock-hewn, burial chambers to the left. As with other rock carvings of this nature in Sardinia, it is known as *domus de janas* which literally translates as 'witches' houses'. In this case, there is a house hewn into one end of the rock outcrop, but this has nothing to do with witches, nor with the original carving of the rock, which dates from prehistoric times.

From Sedini, the road gradually climbs up to a summit, which is

347m (1,138ft) high, and offers views to the coast. The town of **Valledoria** can be seen at the centre of the wide, coastal plain to the right, and the island, Isola Rossa, is visible offshore. The road winds down, through eucalyptus forests, to the hamlet of San Giovanni. One kilometre (½ mile) beyond San Giovanni, on the right of the road, is one of Sardinia's most popular natural monuments, a weathered and worn lump of pinkish-grey rock, known as **L'Elefante**. Its rather vague resemblance to an elephant is best seen from the southern side, a few metres uphill from the lay-by where visitors should park. The trunk hangs over the road and a natural hollow forms a convincing eye. In one side of the rock there are small chambers, hewn from the stone, and as in Sedini, they are known as *domus de janas*, but were originally carved in pre-historic times, probably as burial chambers.

A short distance beyond the elephant rock there is a crossroads. Visitors should continue straight ahead to Castelsardo, which lies 5km (3 miles) further. The road heads between outcrops of dramatic, red rock, which characterises this part of the coast, before **Castelsardo** itself comes into view. The citadel of Castelsardo is picturesquely clustered on a promontory, which has beautiful, deep bays at either side, and an elegant *campanile* at the northernmost tip. A tour of this charming town is the starting point of Route 8a.

Additional Information

Places to Visit

Sassari

Museo Nazionale G.A. Sanna
Via Roma 64
☎ 079 272203
Open: Tuesday to Saturday 9am-2pm, Sunday 9am-1pm. Every second Wednesday of month, 9am-2pm, 4.30-7.30pm.

Mostra Artigianato Sarda
Giardino Pubblico
Open: Monday to Friday 9am-1pm, 4-7.30pm. Saturday and Sunday 9am-1pm.

Santu Antine

Nuraghe Santu Antine
Open: daily, 9am-1pm, 2-6pm.

Torralba

Museo della Valle dei Nuraghi
Vecchia Carlo Felice
☎ 079 847298
Open: winter Tuesday to Sunday 8am-2pm. Summer Tuesday to Sunday 8am-1pm, 2-6pm.

Useful Information

Sassari

Events and Festivals
14 August, I Candelieri. (Religious procession, celebrating the eve of the Assumption, with 3m (10ft) -high candlesticks, which are carved from wood and richly-decorated. Participants wear the traditional, Spanish costumes that would have been worn when the festival celebrated the ending of the plague in 1652).

May, Maggio Sassarese. (During the month of May there is a season of cultural events, including plays, folk displays, exhibitions and sports activities).
Last Sunday of May, La Cavalcata Sarda. (Sardinian folk festival, well-attended by people from all over the island who wear their regional costumes. In the afternoon, there is a Palio, a horse race, and in the evening a Sardinian song and dance display).

Tourist Information Centres
Ente Provinciale per il Turismo
Viale Caprera 36
☎ 079 233751

Azienda Autonoma di Soggiorno e Turismo
Viale Caprera 36
☎ 079 233751

Azienda Autonoma di Soggiorno e Turismo
Via Brigata Sassari 19
☎ 079 231331 or 233534

Transport
Avis (Car Hire)
Via Mazzini 2e
☎ 079 235547

Hertz (Car Hire)
Via IV Novembre 16
☎ 079 280083

Inter Rent (Car Hire)
Viale Caprera 8a
☎ 079 291113

Maggiore (Car Hire)
Viale Italia 3a
☎ 079 235507

Ferrovie dello Stato (State Railway)
Piazza Stazione
☎ 079 260362

Ferrovie Complementari Sarde
(Sardinian Railway)

Via Sicilia 20
☎ 079 241301

Tirrenia Navigazione (Ferry)
Viale Italia 7c
☎ 079 238007 or 230015

ATP (City Bus)
Viale Umberto 139a
☎ 079 274467 or 270098

ARST (Regional Bus)
Emiciclo Garibaldi 15
☎ 079 231449

Strade Ferrate Sarde (Regional Bus)
Emiciclo Garibaldi
☎ 079 241301

PANI Granturismo Autolinee
(Regional Bus)
Via Bellieni 5
☎ 079 236983 or 234782

Taxi Stand
Piazza Castello
☎ 079 234639

Taxi Stand
Emiciclo Garibaldi
☎ 079 234630

Taxi Stand
Piazza Stazione
☎ 079 260150

Travel Agencies
Agitour
Piazza Italia 7
☎ 079 231767

Centro Viaggi Voltaire
Via Arborea 20
☎ 079 234724

Lorviaggi
Viale Dante 14
☎ 079 271489

Oliva
Viale Italia 7c
☎ 079 278007

Sardaviaggi
Via Cagliari 30
☎ 079 234498

Viaggi Quattro Mori
Via Turati 5
☎ 079 210656

Emergencies
Polizia (Police)
Via M. Coppino
☎ 079 232343 or 232332 or 234580

Carabinieri (Military Police)
Via Rockefeller 54
☎ 079 218444

Polizia Stradale (Traffic Police)
Via Genova 26
☎ 079 270080 or 270173

Ospedale Civile (Hospital)
Via E. De Nicola
☎ 079 220500

Ospedale Civile Vecchio (Hospital)
Via E. Costa 57
☎ 079 220820

Ospedale A. Conti (Hospital)
Via Serrasecca
☎ 079 220908

Croce Rossa (Ambulance)
Corso Vico 4
☎ 079 234522

Croce Bianca (Ambulance)
Via San Simplicio 29
☎ 079 275131

Croce Blu (Ambulance)
Via Pietro Micca 7
☎ 079 241113

Croce Verde (Ambulance)
Via Col di lana
☎ 079 242024

Automobile Club d'Italia
Viale Adua 32b
☎ 079 271462 or 272107

8

GALLURA

The region of Gallura has one of the most popular coastlines in Sardinia, as well as a scenic interior that rises up in a multitude of low, rocky crags, from the edge of the dazzling-blue sea. Sea and sand, therefore, are the dominant features of Chapter 8, interspersed with some magnificent coastal scenery and panoramic views. There are umpteen islets and islands scattered offshore, including the French island of Corsica, which can be clearly seen from the northern tip of Gallura. Another interesting coastal feature are the fantastic rock formations that have been sculpted by the elements into forms that seem to take on the characteristics of animals or people. Wind- and sea-weathered rocks, on the headland of Capo Testa, are likened to a human head, and those on Capo d'Orso, to that of a bear. There are other surrealistic rock formations inland, such as the giant mushroom at Arzachena, and no doubt those in the mood can discover many others.

The starting point of Route 8a is the charming, medieval citadel of Castelsardo. The coast south of here is noted for the pinkness of its rock, which reddens to a deep glow at sunset. Route 8b continues along the coast, taking in the offshore islands of Maddalena and Caprera. The latter was the home of the Italian national hero, Garibaldi, and his house is now one of the most popular museums in Italy. Route 8b also travels through the wine-making region of Vermentino di Gallura, a prestigious, dry white wine. Route 8c starts with an inland excursion to the ancient burial grounds, known as the Giants' Graves. Marked by monolithic stones, the tombs date back, some 5,000 years. The remainder of Route 8c, travels along the Emerald Coast, which is the rich-man's playground, developed by multi-millionaire, Agha Khan. Royalty, ambassadors and rock stars are among the clientele here, and luxury yachts fill the harbours.

How much time to allow for each section of Chapter 8 depends very much on how long the visitor spends bathing, as there are numerous optional excursions to beaches. Most of the driving is on winding, coastal roads, but the distances within each route section can be easily covered in a day. Chapter 8 ends at Oblia, which completes this comprehensive, round trip of Sardinia.

Route 8A • Castelsardo to Santa Teresa Gallura

The citadel of **Castelsardo** is perched on the highest point of a promontory, that juts out into the Gulf of Asinara. The road up to the citadel, is marked by yellow signposts to *centro storico*. However, do not try to park inside the citadel walls, where the streets are impossibly narrow, but look for a parking space on the hillside below. There are parking spaces marked along the roadside, and there is also a small parking area at the *belvedere* which is passed on the right. It is not worth proceeding any higher than the *belvedere* by car, as there are no further parking spaces before the citadel walls.

Make the final ascent to the citadel therefore by foot, taking in the good views of the finely constructed, fortified walls, which are built of a severe, dark basalt stone. The walls date from 1102, which was when the powerful merchant family from Genoa, the Dorias, founded the citadel, naming it Castel Genovese. When the Aragonese rose to power, the name was changed to Castel Aragonese. Its present name was given by the House of Savoy in 1769.

Once inside the citadel walls, follow the winding alleys and stairways that lead up to the restored fortress at the top of the town. A portcullised gate leads through the fortress walls to a ticket office. From the ticket office, follow the cobbled passage to the basket-weaving museum. Comprised of two rooms, the collection contains some attractive pieces of local basketware, woven in the traditional manner, with leaves from an indigenous type of dwarf-palm tree. Return to the ticket office, and head up the modern staircase, to the top of the fortress walls. A panoramic terrace offers excellent coastal views, taking in the red-rocked coastline to the east, along with Isola Rossa, and the modern harbour of Castelsardo to the west, as well as the Asinara islands in the distance beyond. On an exceptionally clear day, it is even possible to see Corsica. Closer to hand is the colour-fully-tiled cupola of the duomo and its octagonal *campanile* which is constructed of dark basalt.

To visit the duomo, head back downhill from the fortress, and turn left onto the attractively-paved street, Via Guglielmo Marconi. The

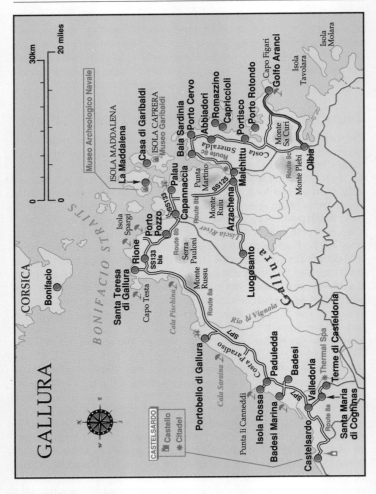

first steps on the right, lead down to the base of the *duomo's campanile*. From here, continue down further steps to the *duomo* façade. Constructed in the sixteenth century, the building has undergone such considerable alteration that little remains of the original Gothic structure. The purpose of visiting the church, however, is to see the beautiful altarpiece, painted by one of the most famous of Sardinia's

(Opposite) The citadel of Castelsardo, perched on a promontory

artists, Maestro di Castelsardo. Contained within an ornate marble surround, the painting is of the *Madonna and Angels*, and depicts the Virgin Mary seated on a throne. The chapels, lining either side of the *duomo's* single aisle, also contain painted altars. There is an attractive, wooden, painted pulpit on the right too.

From the *duomo*, it is possible to walk along the sea walls of the citadel which, being built atop sheer cliffs of trachyte rock, afford refreshing breezes and good views. It is also worth spending time exploring the maze of narrow streets and alleys in the medieval centre. You will find women here sitting on their doorsteps weaving baskets to sell to tourists. Basket-making and textile-weaving are both old traditions of Castelsardo, and although the crafts are now highly commercialised, many of the products are attractive and well-made.

The widest selection of local craft products, including cork and wooden artefacts, is to be had in the large souvenir stores which are on the main road in the modern town of Castelsardo.

Leave Castelsardo by following signs to Valledoria back up to the crossroads, 5km (3 miles) from the town. Turn left at the crossroads onto the SP7. After a short distance, a Nuraghic tower, **Nuraghe Su Tesoru**, is passed to the right of the road. A footpath, of about 50m (55yd), leads up to the mound on which the tower is built. In Nuraghic times the coast was guarded by a series of towers such as this, each having a wide view of the surrounding terrain. Beyond the tower, the road heads down to the wide, coastal plain which surrounds the modern town of **Valledoria**. The town boasts the title, *Citta di Corallo*, and true to its name, there are numerous souvenir shops here, selling coral products. From Valledoria, visitors may wish to make the inland excursion to the thermal spa, **Terme di Casteldoria**. To reach the spa, take the road to Santa Maria Coghinhas, which is 5km (3 miles) south-east of Valledoria. The *terme* (spa) is a further 2km (1 mile) from here, on the slopes of the Anglona hills, and is found by following the appropriate yellow signposts. The spa offers treatments lasting 12 to 14 days for osteoarthritis, rheumatism, respiratory ailments and gynaecological disorders. The waters are prescribed for drinking and bathing in, while other treatment includes massage and physiotherapy.

The route continues through Valledoria, and heads across the plain, which is a patchwork of artichoke fields, to the Coghinas river. At the edge of the plain, where gentle hills sweep up from the flatness, the road climbs up to the small town of **Badesi**. The coast is in sight from here, and a narrow road, signposted *al mare* (to the sea), leads to the beach and campsite at **Badesi Mare**, which is 2km (1

mile) away. Continuing on the SP7, there are scenic coastal views, as
the road winds along the *macchia*-covered hills. Five kilometres (3
miles) north of Badesi, a pleasant excursion can be made to the coast,
by turning left and passing through the modern village
of **Paduledda**. The road continues for a further 4km (2 ½ miles) to the
small resort of **Isola Rossa** and the offshore island of the same name.
Clustered around a pink-rock promontory, the resort is overlooked
by a fat, round tower. To the south of the promontory, is a long sandy
beach, which looks across to the large, but low-lying island, Isola
Rossa, so-named because of its pretty pink rock.

The route proceeds along the SP7, which winds down, offering
views of the jagged, pink-rock cape of Punta li Canneddi, which is
fringed with pretty islets. The same warm, pink rock also dominates
the hinterland, which is gently undulating and covered in *macchia*.
The next stretch of coast, accessible by car, is known as the **Costa
Paradiso** and is signposted on the left. It was named by the specula-
tors who have privatised many of the glorious beaches here and built
discreet holiday villages in the brush. The scenery is worth the 6km
(4 miles) excursion, despite the expanding developments of the
prime spots.

Approximately 5km (3 miles) further north along the SP7, there is
another turning on the left to the coast. The road leads to the beach
of **Cala Saraina**. Those interested in exploring the Costa Paradiso by
horseback can apply to the *maneggio* here, which is on the right,
opposite the turning to Cala Saraina. Perhaps this is a sign of the
exclusivity of the Costa Paradiso, for certainly from this point on, as
far as Olbia, the coast seems to have been bought up by the rich as a
private playground. Camping in the open is strictly prohibited and
private beaches are the norm. The resort of **Portobello di Gallura**,
which is 9km (5 ½ miles) north of Cala Saraina, is a typically select
resort, with wealthy villas built into the hillsides, enjoying the
magnificent vista of the pink-hued coastland and the turquoise sea.

Continuing northwards on the SP7, the route passes through the
prestigious, wine-growing region of **Vermentino di Gallura**. This is
a DOC dry, white wine, which becomes quite strong and rich with
age, but is light and pleasantly fruity when young. Named after the
profusion of vineyards, the road crosses over the Rio di Vignola,
before heading up into a beautiful range of pine-forested hills.
Obscured by the trees, the sea does not come into sight until the
grand, pink-rock cape of Monte Russu, which has a summit of 89m
(292ft). The cape is edged by fine, deserted beaches, the most spectacular of which is at the tip of the promontory, in the shadow of rose-
hued cliffs which redden at sunset, so giving the cape its name. The

Woven textiles at Castelsardo

Many of Sardinia's coastal areas owe their livelihood to fishing

(Opposite) The traditional craft of basket weaving can still be seen throughout Sardinia

beaches are, however, only accessible by foot, and involve a walk through the *macchia* of about 2km (1 mile). The waters here are not very deep, but the current is influenced by the Bonifacio Straits and extra care should be taken if wind-surfing or sailing.

After Monte Russu, the northernmost point of Sardinia, Capo Testa, comes into view, the headland jutting out into the narrow straits. The island of Corsica, with its majestic white cliffs, is clearly visible across the straits. The road continues through pine forests, which sweep down to the water's edge, before briefly joining the coast at a sandy cove. Heading inland once more, the SP7 crosses over two small rivers, Rio Pischina and Rio Sa Faa, after which there is a left turn, marked *spiaggia* (beach). The turning leads through the pine forests, for 800m (850yd), to the popular family beach, **Cala Pischina**. The beach is within 50m (55yd) of the parking area and the water is shallow and safe for children. Those keen on walking may wish to make the scenic hike back from here, along the coast, to the promontory of Monte Russu.

Continuing northwards, the pine forests give way to a boulder-strewn landscape, before reaching the outskirts of Santa Teresa di Gallura, which is the starting point of Route 8b.

Route 8B • Santa Teresa di Gallura to Arzachena

Santa Teresa di Gallura covers a gentle hill, at the northernmost tip of Sardinia, looking across the Bonifacio Straits, to the Corsican town of Bonifacio, which is just 16km (10 miles) away. The regular ferries which ply between the two islands, make the town something of a thoroughfare. However, although it is a place people pass through rather than stop at, the town is attractive in its own right, and has well-equipped beaches nearby, and more around the scenic headland of **Capo Testa**, which is 5km (3 miles) to the west.

To get to Capo Testa, head up to the top of the town, where there is fine, square tower, and turn left. The road heads along the rocky coastline, before dipping down to an isthmus, which links the headland to the mainland. There is a narrow, sandy beach and a small harbour on the right side of the isthmus, which is known as the Baia di Santa Riparta, and a hotel on the other. Continuing onto the headland, the road passes some superb rock formations, the granite worn by the elements into surreal creases and folds, resembling cloth rather than stone. In Roman times, the stone was quarried, and it is known that the granite used for the columns in the Pantheon in Rome, was shipped from the ancient port of *Tibula*, that once stood here, to Ostia. The Pisans also quarried the granite, and used it in the construction of Pisa cathedral. At the tip of the headland there is a lighthouse, from where there are excellent views, both of Corsica and the Sardinian littoral.

From Capo Testa, follow the road back towards Santa Teresa di Gallura, and by-pass the town by forking right at the outskirts. Head for a short distance back along the SP7, before turning left onto the SS133bis, which is signposted to Palau. The road passes within sight of the harbour, to the east of Santa Teresa di Gallura. This narrow creek was once the site of a Roman fortress, although the present-day harbour, which is known as Porto Longosardo, dates from the nineteenth century.

The SS133bis continues through the rocky hills of the hinterland, before reaching a left turn to **La Marmorata** which is one of the finest beaches around Santa Teresa di Gallura. On the opposite side of the turning there is a holiday village, known as **Rione**, which offers horse-riding facilities. Four kilometres (2 miles) further north, along the SS133bis, another left turn leads to the beaches of **La Licciola** and the **Valle dell'Erica**. To the right of the road, rise the craggy hilltops, which culminate in the peak of Serra Pauloni, that has a summit 361m (1,184ft) above sea level. After a further 4km (2 miles), the road passes by the lovely, tree-edged inlet of Porto Pozzo, before tracking inland across the Pozzo river. After a short distance, the first views are afforded of the bare, rocky islands of Spargi and Maddalena. The road then heads down to the Liscia river, before climbing once more through the *macchia*-covered hills to **Capannaccia**. Shortly after Capannaccia, there is a left turn to **Porto Puddu**, where there is a popular wind-surfing centre.

Continuing along the SS133, take the next left turn to **Palau**, which is a good point from which to visit the islands of Maddalena and Caprera. This busy resort, with its attractive, coral-coloured houses and renowned restaurants, surrounds a fishing harbour, to the left side of which is the port from where ferries leave to the islands. Ferries depart every 20 minutes in season, for the 15-minute crossing to the principal island, Maddalena.

The main town on the island, also named **La Maddalena**, is a fashionable resort with elegant architecture. In the excellent maritime museum, the Museo Archeologico Navale, which lies just to the east of the town, the cargo of a second-century BC ship are on display. These, the oldest exhibits in the museum, were found on the sea-bed, between Maddalena and Spargi in 1957, and include wine amphorae, ceramics and statuettes.

There is a panoramic road encircling the island, although the eastern shores are dominated by the unsightly barracks of the Italian

Navy, which are out of bounds. There has been a naval base here since the House of Savoy took control of Sardinia. Nowadays, however, the naval power on the island is somewhat more international, coming, as it does, under the control of N.A.T.O.

A 500m (1,640ft) long causeway connects the island of Maddalena to that of **Caprera**. This barren island is famed for the house in which the Italian national hero, Garibaldi lived. Garibaldi bought the northern part of the island in 1855, and spent his life here as a simple farmer. However, this agrarian lifestyle on the island was periodically interrupted by eccentric campaigns, the most famous of which was in 1861, when Garibaldi marched with his 'thousand', conquering Sicily and Naples. These conquests led to the proclamation of King Vittorio Emanuele, as King of Italy in 1862, although full unification of Italy did not take place until three years later with the surrender of Rome.

Garibaldi's house, the Casa Bianca, is now preserved as a museum, the Museo Garibaldi. It is located just over a kilometre (½ mile) to the east of the causeway and is clearly signposted. Amongst the highlights of a guided tour of the house, are the bed where he slept, his red shirt, and a host of memorabilia, including manifestos and pronouncements, as well as a pair of ivory and gold binoculars that were presented by Edward VII. A clock and calendar mark the time and date of his death and the bed in which he died has also been preserved. The tour ends outside, where Garibaldi's grave is marked by a simple, granite stone, alongside which, stand the more elaborate tombs of his last wife and five children, including his youngest daughter, Clelia. The latter lived on the island up until her death in 1957.

The island is a protected parkland and there is some attractive land to walk around, surrounding Garibaldi's house. It is also possible to see the wall, built by Garibaldi, along the boundary of his property. The other part of the island belonged to an Englishman, named Collins, who was permanently at loggerheads with Garibaldi over his roaming goats. After Collins' death, however, Garibaldi bought the rest of the island, with funds that were collected by a group of English admirers.

The archipelago, of which Maddalena and Caprera are the largest islands, consists of some fifty or more tiny islets. Eons ago, they formed a land bridge, connecting Sardinia and Corsica, until land and sea caused their fragmentation. Boat tours are available around the archipelago, which offers magnificent scenery, sea and beaches.

It is also possible to hire your own boat by applying to Palau Mare which is located in Via Nazionale in the centre of Palau (see Addi-

The surreal mushroom rock formation at Arzachena

tional Information at the end of this chapter).

Capo d'Orso, a beautiful headland, 6km (4 miles) east of Palau, is another popular excursion point from the town. It is usually featured on boat tours from Palau, but it can also be reached by road. It is named after the shape of the rock, at the tip of the promontory, which resembles a bear's head. There are fine views, from here, of both Maddalena and Caprera, as well as the smaller island of San Stefano.

The route continues by climbing back up to the SS133, and proceeding southwards, through the crag-peaked hills of Gallura. The rocky ridge of Punta Martino is passed on the left, and that of Monte Ruiu on the right. The vineyards, growing on the lower slopes, are used in the local production of Vermentino di Gallura. On approaching Arzachena, which is 12km (7 miles) south of Palau, the landscape is strewn with weirdly-eroded boulders and rocks. This rocky terrain surrounds the town of Arzachena, which is the starting point of Route 8c.

Route 8C • Arzachena to Gallura

Follow signs, from the main road, to the *centro storico* of **Arzachena**, passing the little stone church of Santa Lucia, on the left. The centre of the town has rows of attractive houses, painted in tones of coral and amber, but there is little of major interest, as Arzachena is primarily a rather sleepy, agricultural town. However, it is the main commercial centre of the region, and may be useful for its banking and shopping facilities. Arzachena is also a good base from which to make the inland excursion to the giant, burial tombs, the *tombe dei giganti*. There are numerous such tombs throughout Sardinia, but few are as well preserved as those of **Lu Coddu Vecchiu** and **Li Lolghi**, both of which are signposted on the road from Arzachena to Luogosanto. The burial sites are similar in layout, having a central, monumental stele, with a semi-circular opening at the base. The opening leads into a passage, inside which the corpses were buried in a squatting position. Smaller slabs of stone encircle the burial area which would probably have been roofed over. The date of these constructions is unknown, but it is thought that they were probably used during the Nuraghic era which makes them at least 5,000 years old.

Arzachena is also surrounded by fabulous rock formations, some of which have become tourist attractions, due to their uncanny resemblance to real objects. There is the 'mushroom' to the south of the town at the end of Via Limbara, and the 'tortoise' to the north.

From Arzachena, take the SS125, following signs to Costa

Smeralda (Emerald Coast). After 3km (2 miles), the road passes the Nuraghic site of *Malchittu*, on the left, before crossing the Ponte del Mulino. Shortly after the bridge, the route turns left, onto the road to **Baia Sardinia**. It is a winding 11km (7 mile) drive, along the rocky Gulf of Arzachena, to this fashionable holiday resort with its numerous luxury hotels. Continuing along the littoral, the road comes to the **Liscia di Vacca**, a charming bay, overlooked by one of the most exclusive hotel complexes on the Costa Smeralda. Only the elite are welcome, which includes personalities such as Princess Caroline and the King of Jordan.

The **Costa Smeralda**, which is the name given to the coast here, is amongst the most prestigious holiday destinations in Europe. It came into being in the 1960s, when Agha Khan bought 55km (34 miles) of the coast. He had a luxury holiday zone developed, which preserved, as far as possible, the natural beauty of the area. There are no high buildings, no visible wires or cables, no pollution in the sea, and strict planning regulations. The result is a rather artificial landscape, where every bush and tree is neatly ordered. Road signs and hotel hoardings are replaced by discreet granite milestones. Buildings are constructed with natural materials, or are painted in sugary, pastel colours.

Porto Cervo, 2km (1 mile) south of Liscia di Vacca, is the principal resort on the Emerald Coast, and surrounds the best-protected, natural harbour in Sardinia. Life here, centres around the marina, which is full of luxury yachts, including that of Gianni Agnelli, the owner of Fiat and one of the wealthiest men in Italy. During the day, yacht-owners sail out to the many beautiful coves and beaches that are dotted along the Emerald Coast, reaching spots that are neither serviced by public ferries nor are accessible by road. In the evenings, the *piazetta* (small square) comes to life, and the salubrious restaurants throng with a well-dressed crowd. Gawping, or spending enormous sums of money, which includes going to the shopping arcade where Gucci, Cartier and other top labels are represented, are the main things to do in Porto Cervo. The only monument of any interest is the little church of Stella Maris which stands on the hill above the resort. It was built in the 1970s to a design by the Roman architect, Michel Busiri Vici. Inside, there is a painting by El Greco of the *Madonna*, which was donated by one of the church's wealthy patrons. There is also a fine, sixteenth-century organ from Naples, and a valuable altar cross from Germany.

The route continues south of Porto Cervo, climbing up through the *macchia*-covered hills to **Abbiadori**. From here, the road descends once more to the coast, where excursions can be made to some of the more popular beaches on the Emerald Coast. Take the small road to Cala di Volpe, where the famous Pevero Golf Course is idyllically located above the bay. There is a fine beach at **Capriccioli**, the nearby resort, but the more impressive beach, is that of **Romazzino**, which is a further 2km (1 mile) along the coast. Guarded by high security police and private body guards, the beach looks out to a cluster of islets, the nearest of which is Isola Soffi.

The route continues southwards, along the Emerald Coast, from where a fine panorama is afforded of both the nearby islets and the high-cliffed cape of Golfo Aranci, as well as the vast walls of the Tavolara island beyond. The beautiful bay of Cala di Volpe stretches below, with its luxury villas built into the hillside. The scenery inland is a mass of craggy peaks, amongst the tallest of which, is Punta Cugnana which is 649m (2,128ft) high. The coast is not accessible again, until reaching **Portisco**, which is reached by turning left off the main road. This modern resort lies at the southernmost tip of the Emerald Coast. It has a fine position at the edge of the Gulf of Cugnana, at the other side of which lies Porto Rotondo.

The road continues alongside the gulf which is unusually deep and narrow, and is overlooked by mushrooming holiday villas, painted in the obligatory sunset colours. After passing by the mouth of the gulf, where the waters are very shallow, the road heads between the rocky ridge of Monte Sa Curi, which is 415m (418ft) high, to the left, and the isolated peak of Monte Plebi, which has a summit of 473m (1,551ft), to the right. A turning on the left, leads to the resort of **Porto Rotondo**, which lies just outside the official Emerald Coast zone, and to **Golfo Aranci**.

Golfo Aranci is a port town, located at the foot of the rocky cape, Capo Figari. There are daily ferries from here, to Civitavecchia and Livorno, on the Italian mainland. Otherwise, the town has little to offer, although there are some fine beaches surrounding the cape, which are particularly popular for sub-aqua diving. Just off the northern tip of the cape, is the uninhabited island of Figarolo, which shelters a surviving herd of moufflon sheep. For a panoramic view of this island, and the surrounding coasts, take the road up to the top of Capo Figari, where there is a disused lighthouse.

From Golfo Aranci, it is a scenic 18km (11 miles) drive, along the rocky coastline, to Olbia. Visitors leaving Sardinia by ferry from here, will find the port without difficulty, as it is well signposted, one only needs to follow the ferry symbol.

Additional Information

Places to Visit

Caprera
Museo Garibaldi
Open: Tuesday to Saturday 9am-
1.30pm. Sunday 9am-12.30pm.

Castelsardo
Castello
Open: daily 9am-7pm.

Sardartis
Mostra Mercato (Craft Market)
Via Sedini
☎ 079 470388 or 470366

La Maddalena
Museo Archeologico Navale
Open: Monday to Saturday 9am-
12noon.

Terme di Casteldoria
Terme di Casteldoria (Thermal Spa)
☎ 079 585601
Open: May to November.

Useful Information

Arzachena
Tourist Information Centre
Azienda Autonoma di Soggiorno e
    Turismo
Piazza Risorgimento
☎ 0789 82624

Travel Agencies
CO.SI.CA.
Via Costa Smeralda 53
☎ 0789 82557

Agenzia Viaggi e Turismo
Viale Costa Smeralda 186
☎ 0789 82557

Emergencies
Carabinieri (Military Police)
☎ 0789 82062

Guardia Medica (Medical Officer)
☎ 0789 82581

Baia Sardinia
Transport
Avis (Car Hire)
Via Tre Monti
☎ 0789 99139

Noleggio Imbarcazioni (Boat Hire)
Centro Servizi Nautici
Poltu Quatu
☎ 0789 99433

Travel Agencies
Smeral Tours
Piazzetta
☎ 0789 99092

Unimare
Piazzetta Centrale
☎ 0789 99144

Emergencies
Medical Service
Servizi Polispecialistici
Bivio Baia Sardinia
☎ 0789 99750

Caprera
Sports Facilities
Centro Velico (Sailing Centre)
Punta Coda
☎ 0789 77791

Castelsardo
Events and Festivals
Easter Monday, Lunissanti.
(Medieval-origin procession by
candlelight, participants sing the
Gregorian chant).

2 August, Madonna degli Angeli.
(Festival celebrated with entertainments and folk dancing).

Tourist Information Centre
Pro Loco
Piazza del Popolo
☎ 079 470585

Travel Agencies
Sea Gull Travel
Via Veneto 5
☎ 079 470495

Emergencies
Carabinieri (Military Police)
☎ 079 470122

Guardia Medica (Medical Officer)
Via Colombo
☎ 079 470272

La Maddalena
Tourist Information Centre
Azienda Autonoma di Soggiorno e
   Turismo
Via XX Settembre 24
☎ 0789 736321

Transport
Tirrenia Navigazione (Ferry)
Via Amendola 10a
☎ 0789 737660

Travel Agencies
Isolana Viaggi
Via Amendola 10
☎ 0789 737660

Unimare
Via Garibaldi 56
☎ 0789 738668

Emergencies
Carabinieri (Military Police)
☎ 0789 737004

Guardia Medica (Medical Officer)
☎ 0789 738288

Pronto Soccorso (First Aid Service)
☎ 0789 737497

Ospedale di La Maddalena
   (Hospital)
Via Ammirale Magnaghi
☎ 0789 737751

Automobile Club d'Italia
Via Fratelli Bandiera 1
☎ 0789 737484

Palau
Tourist Information Centre
Azienda Autonoma di Soggiorno e
   Turismo
Via Nazionale 94
☎ 0789 709570

Transport
Tirrenia Navigazione (Ferry)
Piazza del Molo
☎ 0789 70920

Noleggio Imbarcazione (Boat Hire)
Via Fonte Vecchia 76
☎ 0789 709780

Consorzio Operatori Marittimi
(Boat Hire & Tours)
Porto Turistico
☎ 0789 709743

Travel Agencies
Aquarius Travel
Via Nazionale 2
☎ 0789 709676

Avitours
Via de Martis
☎ 0789 709530

Unimare
Via Fontevecchia 76
☎ 0789 709260

Emergencies
Carabinieri (Military Police)
☎ 0789 709503

Medical Service
Servizi Polispecialistici
☎ 0789 700000

Porto Cervo
Sports Facilities
Pevero Golf Club
☎ 0789 96210

Cervo Tennis Club
☎ 0789 92244

Transport
Avis (Car Hire)
Piazza Clipper
☎ 0789 91244

Eurorent (Car Hire)
Sottopiazza
☎ 0789 94263

Noleggio Imbarcazioni (Boat Hire)
La Compagnia dell'Avventura
Villagio Alba Ruja
☎ 0789 91724

Travel Agencies
Sardinia International Travel
Piazza Centrale
☎ 0789 92225

Emergencies
Polizia (Police)
☎ 0789 91666

Carabinieri (Military Police)
☎ 0789 92028

Medical Service
Bivio Porto Cervo
☎ 0789 99750

Santa Teresa di Gallura
Events and Festivals
September, National Horse Race.

Tourist Information Centre
Azienda Autonomo di Turismo
Piazza Vittorio Emanuele 24
☎ 0789 754127

Transport
Tirrenia Navigazione (Ferry)
Via del Porto
☎ 0789 74156

NAV.AR.MAR. (Ferry)
Via del Porto
☎ 0789 755260

Travel Agencies
Agenzie Marittime Sarde
Piazza del Porto 15
☎ 0789 754788

Sardinia Tours
Via XX Settembre 14
☎ 0789 754356

Agenzia di Viaggi e Turismo
Piazza Villamarina 1
☎ 0789 754464

Emergencies
Polizia (Police)
☎ 0789 754122

Guardia Medica (Medical Officer)
Via Enrico Berlinguer
☎ 0789 754079

Automobile Club d'Italia
Via Genova 4
☎ 0789 754077

Sardinia: Fact File

Accommodation

Agriturismo

The Agriturismo scheme gives tourists the opportunity to stay with a Sardinian family, in a farmhouse, tucked away in the countryside. Traditional Sardinian hospitality, makes this a pleasurable experience, as well as offering an insight into the everyday, rural life of the island.

The tariffs for this type of accommodation are generally fixed by an agritourism organisation and do not fluctuate with the seasons. The visitor has the choice of *mezza pensione* (half-board) or *pernottamento e prima colazione* (bed and breakfast). Most establishments also offer a weekend package, *week-end completo*, which starts with the Friday evening meal and ends with Sunday lunch.

The standard of accommodation varies from being a simple bed and breakfast arrangement, to a small, country hotel organisation. The latter often organise excursions to places of interest in the surrounding region, and may have sports facilities, such as horse-riding, tennis or swimming.

There are some 200 Agriturismo establishments in Sardinia that are affiliated with a national group. To give an idea of the range of Agriturismo accommodations, below is a brief outline of a selection of establishments in each of Sardinia's four provinces.

Cagliari

The Cooperativa Agricola Matteu, based in Teulada, is affiliated with the Agriturist organisation. The farm is set in 450 hectares (1,111 acres) of vineyards and olive groves, and guests can participate in work on the farm. Excursions on foot, horseback or by Landrover are also offered.

Pierpaolo Piga, in Capoterra, is affiliated with Terra Nostra. It is located in the countryside 3km (2 miles) from the sea. The farm specialises in greenhouse cultivation, including tropical plants. Tours and horseback excursions are offered on Monte Arcosu, a nearby mountain which is covered in beautiful forests.

Oristano

The Cooperativa Allevatrici Sarde, which is based in Santa Lucia-Zeddiani, is affiliated with Agriturist, and was one of the first agritourism ventures in Sardinia. The cooperative is made up of 80 farms, distributed among 16 villages, in the province of Oristano. The farms offer simple, traditional fare and the possibility of visiting the surrounding churches, Nuraghic sites and archaeological remains.

The Azienda Agricola Vincenzo Grussu, located near Morgongiori, is affiliated with Turismo Verde. This friendly farm is surrounded by 30 hectares (74 acres) of land, part of which is cultivated with fruit orchards. Excursions are offered to nearby Monte Arci, as well as to the coast.

Lucia Sotgiu, at Nurachi, is affiliated with Terra Nostra. This historic, Sardinian house is preserved with its original decor and furnishings. Visitors are given an insight into traditional, Sardinian life, and are offered all home-produced fare, including local breads and liqueurs.

Nuoro

The Azienda Agricola Testone is based in Nuoro and is affiliated with Agriturist. It is a large farm, with 270 hectares (667 acres) of land, and offers guests a wide variety of home-produced fare, including yoghurt, cheese, milk, lamb, veal and honey. It also has facilities for horseriding.

Sassari

The Cooperativa Agricola Sa Giorba is located at Santa Maria La Palma, a short distance from the coast, and is affiliated with Turismo Verde. The farm cultivates grain, vegetables and fruit. It also has stables and horseriding facilities.

Stazzo Le Querce, a historic perfume distillery, is situated near Baia Sardinia and is affiliated with Agriturist. Perfumes and essences are still produced here, and the farm grows its own aromatic herbs and flowers. It offers courses to guests in the traditional methods of perfume distillation and aromatherapy.

For further information contact the organising bodies of agritourism in Sardinia at the address below. These organisations should also be contacted for reservations, which must be made in advance. Reservations are made by placing an advance for the sum of 30 per cent of the total expected cost per person.

Terranostra	Turismo Verde	Agriturist
Via Sassari 3	Via Libeccio 31	Via Trieste 6
Cagliari	Cagliari	Cagliari
☎ 070 668367	☎ 070 373733	☎ 070 668330

Camping

Camping is a major part of the Italian tourist industry and all tourist offices hold details of local sites. Federcampeggio, the Italian Camping Federation, publishes two lists of campsites, which cover the whole of Italy, including Sardinia. The first of these is a comprehensive list with details of all the sites, which costs around £10 (US$17). The second is a more abbreviated list which is issued free. Either list may be obtained from:

Centro Internazionale Prenotazioni
Federcampeggio
Casella Postale 23
50041 Calenzano (FI)
☎ 055 882391

There is also a yearbook, called the *Annuario Campeggio*, published by ESIT (Ente Sardo Industrie Turistiche), which lists the main campsites in Sardinia. The campsites are graded according to their facilities and position. The booklet is available free of charge from the following address:

Ente Sardo Industrie Turistiche
Via Mameli 97
Cagliari
☎ 070 60231

Most of Sardinia's campsites are well-equipped and often have bars, restaurants, tennis courts, discos and children's play areas. During July and August, the camping grounds are very busy with holidaymakers from the mainland as well as French, Swiss and Germans. The majority of campsites are to be found along the north and north-west coast, although campsites are dotted around all the principal coastal resorts. Inland, there are no camping facilities. It may seem tempting to camp in the open here, as there are many ideal locations. However, free-camping is against the law, and locals do not recommend it due to the possibility of theft or attack. The interior of Sardinia has something of a reputation for unruly shepherds and even bandits.

Hotels

Hotels are generally classified on a star system, which ranges from one to five. The prices a hotel charges depends on its classification and on the season, the peak season running from 1 July to 1 September, and also a week each at Christmas and Easter time. The prices are fixed, and should be displayed in each room. Hotels at the lower end of the market are generally known as *albergo* and *pensione*. The same rule applies regarding tariffs. In cities and in the more popular resorts it is possible to find *camere*, rooms to rent, which are the cheapest type of accommodation. Again the prices are fixed, unless the establishment is not officially registered, in which case charges are open to bargaining.

Hotel reservations cannot be made through ENIT (Ente Nazionale Italiano per il Turismo), the Italian National Tourist Office abroad, although they do hold lists of organisations who can book hotels (normally 4 or 5 star) in all major tourist areas. In Italy, EPT (Ente Provinciale per il Turismo), APT (Azienda di Promozione Turistica) or AA (Azienda Autonoma di Soggiorno e Turismo), which are the tourist offices found in most Italian towns, and the Pro Loco offices found in smaller centres, hold comprehensive lists of local hotels and *pensione*, and some will actually phone and book rooms for visitors. Most of the larger offices will supply accommodation lists on written request. The *Annuario Alberghi*, published by ESIT (Ente Sardo Industrie Turistiche), is a year book of hotels in Sardinia. The hotels that are listed range from one- to five-star and information is provided regarding facilities and tariffs. The booklet is available free of charge from the following address:

Ente Sardo Industrie Turistiche
Via Mameli 97
Cagliari ☎ 070 60231

Mountain Refuges

The mountain huts in Sardinia are run by the Club Alpino Italiano. They are very basic, usually with a dormitory and some simple cooking facilities, and are only of interest to hikers. They are not open on a regular basis therefore bookings must be made in advance. For further information and reservations contact the addresses below:

Club Alpino Italiano
Via Ugo Foscolo
Milano
☎ 02 802554 or 8057519

Club Alpino Italiano
Via Principe Amedeo 25
Cagliari
☎ 070 667877

Youth Hostels
It is not necessary to belong to a youth hostelling association in order to stay at hostels in Sardinia. However, visitors are recommended to make bookings in advance, particularly for August. During the off-peak season, it is advisable to check the hostel is open, as this tends to be the time when maintenance and re-decorating takes place. The addresses of the only three Youth Hostels in Sardinia are as follows:

Ostello dei Giuliani
Via Zara 1
Fertilia
Alghero
☎ 079 930353

Ostello Balai
Via Lungomare 91
Porto Torres
☎ 079 502761

Ostello Eleonora d'Arborea
Via dei Pescatori 31
Torre Grande
☎ 0783 22097

Associazion Italiana Alberghi
per la Gioventu
Comitato Regionale
Via Giudice Ugone 1
Cagliari ☎ 070 42796 or ☎ 808138

Additional Information

This section appears at the end of each chapter and is comprised of two parts: Places to Visit and Useful Information. Information includes local events and festivals, addresses and opening times of places of interest, sports facilities, transport services, travel agencies and emergency contact and tourist information centres. The information is listed under town names, in alphabetical order.

Where applicable, opening times for museums and monuments are given for the summer season, which runs from 1 June to 30 September, and for the winter season, which starts on 1 October and ends on 30 May. Opening times are also

Maximum and minimum daily temperatures

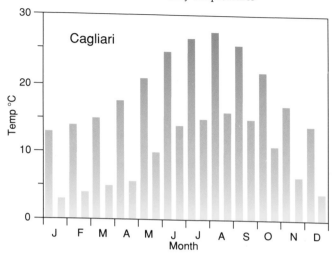

Average monthly rainfall

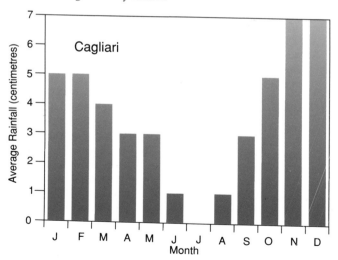

given for holidays, which include Sundays, public holidays and local closing days. Opening times change slightly from year to year, but they will be substantially as stated.

Churches are generally open from 7am until midday. They open again for afternoon mass and generally close around sunset. Visitors should dress with due respect and take care not to interrupt a service. Churches that are not in regular use are kept locked. It is possible to get inside by finding the church warden who generally lives nearby. Alternatively, apply to the local *comune*, town hall, or tourist office.

Climate

Sardinia's climate is typical of the Mediterranean, having mild winters and long, hot summers which generally last from May until October. The south experiences slightly higher temperatures than the north of the island, while the lowest temperatures are to be found in the mountainous interior, where snow caps the highest peaks from November to March. The average temperatures for December are: 10°C (50°F) in Sassari and 12°C (54°F) in Cagliari. In July the average temperature in Sassari is 24°C (75°F) and in Cagliari it is 26°C (79°F).

Due to its exposed nature as an island, Sardinia is prone to strong winds all year round. The most common wind is the *maestrale* (mistral) which blows from the north-west. In the winter, the *maestrale* lowers the temperatures, while in the summer it carries pockets of hot air which raise the temperatures quite dramatically. This wind blows so frequently that the trunks of trees and plants are invariably bent towards the south-east. In the south of the island and on the west coasts the *libeccio* wind carries rain. The warm *scirocco*, known locally as the *levante*, also blows in the southern parts of Sardinia, particularly on the south-eastern coast.

When to visit Sardinia, depends on the type of holiday you want. July and August, the busiest months, find resorts in full swing, with a wide variety of entertainment, including local festivals, exhibitions and concerts. The heat and the crowds subside by mid-September and many hotels and restaurants gradually close down for the winter. There are very few tourists during the winter months, and although facilities are therefore limited, the island is peaceful and by January the almond blossom and the first flowers are already starting to bud. For a real spread of colour, visit Sardinia in the early spring, when temperatures may just be warm enough to swim. The average water temperature in April is 14°C (57°F). It reaches up to 24°C (75°C) in August and is still 21°C (70°F) in October.

Credit Cards

All major credit cards (Access, American Express, Visa etc) are taken at most large restaurants, hotels and shops. Eurocheques and traveller's cheques are also usually accepted. The notable exceptions are filling stations, which tend to only accept cash. In the less-frequented parts of Sardinia, it is also useful to have a certain amount of cash on hand as services seen throughout the rest of the island may not exist.

Currency Regulations

The Italian monetary unit is the Lira (plural Lire). No traveller may import or export more than 500,000 Lire in cash, although unlimited amounts of sterling, dollars or traveller's cheques are permitted. It is advisable to check the current situation as the regulations will undoubtedly change.

Customs Regulations

Normal EEC Customs regulations apply. The Italian age limit for the import of duty-free alcohol and tobacco is 17. Normal personal equipment — cameras, jewellery etc — can be taken into the country, but it is advisable to record all serial numbers and keep receipts for valuable items. If it is not possible to provide a receipt, a photocopy or a photograph will suffice. Any articles purchased in Italy, which exceed the custom's allowance set by your country, are liable for duty.

No visa is required for stays of less than 3 months for holders of passports issued by the EEC, Britain, Ireland, Canada or the United States, but a valid passport is required.

Electricity

The electricity is 220 volts AC, 50 Hertz (cycles per second). Four different types of plug are commonly used — two with two pins and two with three pins in a line. While a two-pin continental adaptor is recommended, purchasing plugs on arrival is easy and inexpensive.

Embassies and Consulates

Foreign Embassies in Rome
Australia
Via Alessandria 215
☎ 06 832721

Canada
Via Zara 30
☎ 06 8441841

UK
Via XX Settembre 80a
☎ 06 4755441

USA
Via Veneto 119a
☎ 06 4674

Foreign Consular Offices in Sardinia

UK
Via San Lucifero 87
Cagliari
☎ 070 662755

Emergency Services

For Fire, Police and Ambulance, ring 113. For immediate attention at airports, main railway stations and hospitals, look for the *pronto soccorso*, first aid service. For emergency road breakdowns call 116. The *soccorso stradale*, breakdown service, is a nationwide facility, operated by ACI, the Automobile Club d'Italia.

Health Care

British and Irish travellers have a right to claim health services in Italy by virtue of EEC regulations. Form E111, available from the Department of Social Security, should be obtained before leaving Britain. Italian health services are administered by USL (Unita Sanitaria Locale). The local USL authorities will advise visitors where and how to go about receiving treatment. For more urgent matters go directly to the nearest hospital. Doctors' surgeries are usually busy and the waiting rooms operate on a first come, first served basis.

American and Canadian tourists will need to check the validity of their personal health insurance to ensure they are adequately covered.

Drugs that are prescribed by a doctor and dispensed at a pharmacy (*farmacia*), are liable for a minimal local tax, which will not be reimbursed. The *farmacia* always has a list of pharmacies open at night, and on Sundays, and other normal closing times.

Hikers are advised to purchase *siero anti vipera* to add to their first aid kit. This is a vaccine to be taken after snakebites and is available over the counter in most Italian pharmacies.

Holidays and Festivals

Shops, banks, offices, schools and some museums are closed for the national holidays as below.

New Year's Day
Epiphany (6 January)
Easter Monday
Liberation Day (25 April)
Labour Day (1 May)
Republic Day (2 June)
Assumption *Ferragosto* (15 August)
All Saints Day *Ognissanti* (1 November)
Immaculate Conception (8 December)
Christmas Day (25 December)
St Stephen's Day (26 December)

Every city, town and village in Sardinia also closes for their local festival days. These are mostly listed under Events and Festivals in the Additional Information section at the end of each chapter. Those interested in finding out more about Sardinian festivals can apply for the free publication, *1000 Feste*, which is produced by ESIT (see Tourist Information for address).

Language

Sardinian and Dialect

Italian is the official language of Sardinia. However, Sardinian, which is a Latin-based language, is also spoken throughout the island with regional variations. The dialect of Logudoro, is generally considered the most pure form, and is spoken in the northern central part of the island. That known as Campidania is spoken in the southern regions. In the mountainous regions around Nuoro, the dialects are diverse and have ancient origins. The dialects of Sassarese and Gallurese reveal the influences of Corsican and Tuscan, and as testimony to the 400-year rule of the Spanish, a form of Catalan is still spoken in Alghero. Another linguistic oasis is the island of San Pietro. Settled by Ligurians in 1736, a form of Ligurian dialect is still spoken here.

Italian

Italian is a straightforward language in which words are written as they are pronounced, and each letter has only one sound (except for the letters e, o, c and g which have two each).

The basic pronunciation rules are as follows:

c before *e* or *i* is pronounced *ch* (as in cheese) eg. *vicino* (near) veecheeno

elsewhere *c* is pronounced as in cat eg. *camera* (bedroom)

ch is pronounced *k* eg. *perche* (why/because) pairkay

e is pronounced either as in hen or as the *a* in day eg. *ecco* (here) echo or *che* (what) kay

g before *e* and *i* is pronounced *j* eg. *Germania* (Germany) jairmarnia

elsewhere *g* is hard eg. *grosso* (big)

gl is pronounced *ly* eg. *aglio* (garlic) alyoe

gn is pronounced *nye* as at the beginning of new eg. *gnomo* (gnome) nye-omo

h is silent eg. *ha* (has) a

sc before *e* and *i* is pronounced *sh* eg. *fascismo* (fascism) fasheezmoe

elsewhere *sc* is pronounced *sk* eg *tasca* (pocket) taska

z and *zz* are pronounced *ts* or *ds* (*dz*), although this tends to vary according to the local dialect, eg. *mezza* (medza)

Basic Vocabulary

si — yes (see)

no — no

per favore or *per piacere* — please

grazie — thank you (grat-see-ay)

prego — don't mention it (pray-go)

va bene — all right (va bayney)

buongiorno — good morning (bwon-jorno)

buona sera — good afternoon/good evening (bwona saira)

buona notte — good night (bwona nottay)

dov'é — where is? (dough-vey)

quando? — when? (kwan-dough)

che cosa? — what? (kay koza)

quanto? — how much? (kwan-toe)

quanto costa? — how much does it cost? (kwan-toe kosta)

parla Inglese — do you speak English (parla inglaysay)

non capisco — I don't understand (known capee-sko)

posso avere — can I have? (posso av-ay-ray)

vorrei — I would like (vorray)

mi scusi — excuse me (me skuzee)

aperto — open (a-pair-toe)

chiuso — closed (queue-zoe)

caldo — hot (cal-doe)

freddo — cold (fray-doe)

grande — large (grand-day)

piccolo — small (pronounced as the instrument)

buono — good (bwon-oh)

cattivo — bad (ca-teevoe)

invernale — winter (in-ver-narlay)

estate — summer (e-start-ay)

festivo — holiday (fest-ee-voe)

feriale — working day (fair-ee-arlay)

cambio — currency exchange (cam-bee-oh)

Numbers

zero — 0	*cinque* — 5
uno — 1	*sei* — 6
due — 2	*sette* — 7
tre — 3	*otto* — 8
quattro — 4	*nove* — 9

dieci — 10
venti — 20
trenta — 30
quaranta — 40
cinquanta — 50
sessanta — 60
settanta — 70
ottanta — 80
novanta — 90
cento — 100

duecento — 200
mille — 1,000
duemila — 2,000
tremila — 3,000
un milione — 1,000,000
un miliardo — 1,000,000,000
primo — first
secondo — second
terzo — third

Hotel Vocabulary

una camera — a room
due, tre camere — two, three rooms
con bagno — with bathroom (cone banyoe)
con doccia — with shower (cone dot-chee-ah)
giorni — days (jor-knee)
una settimana — a week (oona set-tim-arna)
la colazione — breakfast (col-lats-ee-oh-nay)
la cena — evening meal (latchaynah)

Motoring Vocabulary

Alt — Stop
Accendere i Fari in Galleria — Use Headlights in Tunnel
Tenere la Destra (Sinistra) — Keep Right (Left)
Divieto di Sosta (or Sosta Vietata) — No Parking
Avanti — Walk (at pedestrian crossings)
Entrata — Entrance
Uscita — Exit
Lavori in Corso — Roadworks Ahead
Passaggio a Livello — Level Crossing
Pericolo — Danger
Rallentare — Slow Down
Polizia Stradale — Traffic Police
Senso Unico — One Way Street
Senso Vietato — No entry
Divieto di Sorpasso — No Overtaking
Sosta Autorizzato — Parking Allowed (within stated times)
Strada Senza Uscita — Cul-de-sac
Passo Carrabile — Thoroughfare in use — no waiting
Vicolo Cieco — No Through Road

Zona Pedonale — Pedestrian Zone
Strada Privata — Private Road
Parcheggio — Carpark
Alt Stazione — Toll Booth

Restaurant Vocabulary
Il conto — The bill
La lista — The menu
Vino Bianco — White wine
Vino Rosso or *Vino Nero* — Red wine
Vino della casa — House wine, order this by the *litro* or
   mezzo litro (litre or half litre)
Servizio Commpreso — Service charge included
Acqua minerale gassata — Fizzy mineral water
Acqua minerale non gassata — Still mineral water

Sightseeing Vocabulary
Duomo/Cattedrale — Cathedral
Chiesa — Church
Campanile — Bell tower
Chiostro — Cloisters
Tomba — Tomb
Pinacoteca — Picture Gallery
Museo — Museum
Palazzo — Mansion, important building
Centro Storico — Historic Centre
Castello — Castle
Rocca — Fortress

Medical Vocabulary
dolore — pain
mal di pancia — stomach ache
diarrea — diarrhoea
mal di testa — headache
mal di denti — toothache
febbre — fever
influenza — flu
cerotto — band aid
raffreddore — a cold
tosse — cough
dolore al petto — chest pain
pressione alta — high blood pressure
ricetta — prescription

Glossary of Classical Architecture

Agora — Greek market place (Roman *forum*)
Atrium — courtyard at entrance of a Roman House
Cavea — seating area of a classical theatre
Cella — inner sanctuary in a temple
Impluvium — basin to collect rain water
Nymphaeum — monumental fountain
Peristyle — inner courtyard, surrounded by colonnades
Pronaos — porch of a temple

Maps

Touring Club Italiano produce a good 1:200,000 scale map of Sardinia. The island is also included on national maps of Italy, such as Bartholomew's 1:1,000,000 easy fold map, which is handy for navigating, and the Michelin map of the same scale, which is clear and reliable. For hikers, the best maps are those produced by the Istituto Geografico Militario. They cover relatively small areas, but show a good amount of detail, which is essential since footpaths are generally poorly marked. They vary in scale from 1:25,000 to 1:100,000 and are only available from specialist map shops. Most of the local tourist offices in Italy issue free maps of individual provinces, as well as town plans.

Measurements

The metric system is used in Italy. Conversions are:

1 kilogram (1,000 grams) = 2.2lb
1 litre = 1 3/4 pints
4.5 litres = 1 gallon
8km = 5 miles

Weights of food are often measured by the *etto* which is the equivalent of 100g. The plural of *etto* is *etti*. If you want 200g of salami, ask for *due etti di salami*.

Money

Money can be changed at *cambio* (exchange) offices in major towns and resorts, and banks elsewhere. It is normal procedure to show your passport, and all receipts should be kept.

All Italian banks have a cashier which means that the transaction is made on paper at the regular desk, while the actual money is collected at the *cassa* (cash desk). Always allow plenty of time for changing money, as banks invariably have slow-moving queues.

Banks are normally open between 8.30am and 12.30pm, and usually for an hour in the afternoon, between 3pm and 4pm, Monday to Friday only.

The largest denomination of Lire is the 500,000L note; which is roughly equivalent to £250. There are also 100,000L, 50,000L, 10,000L, 5,000L, 2,000L and 1,000L notes. The biggest denomination coin is the 500L. There are also 200L, 100L and 50L coins.

Police

The police force is made up of various different branches. The *Carabinieri* are a semi-military police force who take care of civilian disturbances. Their telephone number is posted at the outskirts of every town. The *Vigili Urbani* and the *Polizia Urbani* take care of everyday problems. The *Polizia Stradale*, deal with traffic accidents and any road problems. While driving around Sardinia it is quite normal to be stopped by police at the road side. These are routine checks and are carried out by any of the police branches, as well as the *Guardia di Finanzia* who, in addition to requesting the regular circulation documents, insurance, driving licence and proof of identity, may ask to see receipts for any purchases in the car. This explains the Italian diligence in issuing receipts for even the most insignificant purchases.

All tourists must register with the police within 3 days of entering the country. If you stay at a hotel, campsite etc. this will be carried out for you.

Post and Telephone Services

Stamps (*francoboli*) are sold at both post offices and tobacconists. Post offices are normally open from: 8.30am to 1.30pm, Monday to Friday; and 8.30am to 12.30pm on Saturdays. Central post offices in larger towns generally offer postal services up until 7 or 8pm.

Tobacconists (*tabaccherie*), recognised by the 'T' sign in front of their shop, are normally open from 8.30am to 1pm, and 3.30pm to 8pm, Monday to Saturday.

Public telephones take coins of 100, 200 and 500 Lire, as well as *gettoni* (200 Lire tokens). *Gettoni* are available at tobacconists, bars or new stands, and are sometimes given as change. Many public phones take magnetic phone cards, which can be purchased, for 5,000 or 10,000 Lire, at airports, railway stations, public phone offices (SIP) and authorised vendors. Bars often have *telefoni a scatti* (telephones with a meter) which record the number of units for each call. This avoids the need to be continually feeding in small change, but the bar price usually includes a small surcharge. In larger towns, SIP (Societa Italiana Telefoni), the Italian Telephone Company, provide soundproof booths with meters.

International dialling codes from Italy are:

Great Britain 0044
Canada 001
USA 001
Australia 0061

Remember to leave out the first zero of your home country number — eg to dial the Italian Tourist Office in London (071 4081254) from Italy dial 0044 71 4081254.

Photography

All types of film are readily available in Italy, but prices vary and are generally more expensive in popular tourist centres. In many museums and churches it is forbidden to use tripods or flash, so it is well-worth purchasing a 1000 ASA film when planning to visit indoor sights, although in summer any film faster than 200 ASA will make outdoor photography difficult.

Tipping

Service charges of 15 per cent and IVA (VAT) of 19 per cent are included on most restaurant and hotel bills. However, it is normal to give an extra 5 per cent of the bill for satisfactory service. The same is also true for cafés and bars, particularly in the more upmarket places. Remember that in Italy there is also a table charge for sitting in a café, which can double the bill in popular tourist spots. Cinema and theatre usherettes expect small tips, and porters are generally tipped about 1,000 Lire per suitcase. Other people you might expect to tip are washroom attendants and serve station attendants who clean the windscreen. Taxi drivers expect a tip of 10 per cent and tourist guides are normally tipped 1,000 Lire per person.

Tourist Information Centres

The tourist offices in large towns are run by Ente Provinciale per il Turismo, which hold tourist information on the province, and Azienda Autonoma di Soggiorno e Turismo, which offer assistance with accommodation as well as having local information for tourists. In smaller places, there is usually a Pro Loco office, which provides local information only. The quality of service available from these tourist offices is variable, but the vast majority are helpful.

Tourist Information Centres Overseas

UK
1 Princes Street
London W1R 8AY
☎ (071) 408 1254

USA
630 Fifth Avenue
Suite 1565 Rockefeller
    Centre
New York NY10111
☎ (212) 245 4961 or 4822

500 North Michigan
Avenue
Suite 1046
Chicago IL 60611
☎ (312) 644 0990

360 Post Street
Suite 801
San Francisco CA 94109
☎ (415) 392 6206

Canada
Store 56
Plaza
3 Place Ville Marie
Montreal
Quebec H3B 2E3
☎ (514) 866 7667 or
7668 or 7669

Travel

Air

Cagliari, Olbia and Alghero have the main international airports in Sardinia. The airport at Cagliari, known as Elmas Aeroporto, is a 15-minute drive from the city centre, and is connected by a regular bus shuttle service. Olbia's airport, which is 3km (2 miles) from the town, is called Costa Smeralda Aeroporto and also operates a bus shuttle service. Fertilia Aeroporto, which is 7km (4 miles) from Alghero and 35km (22 miles) from Sassari does not offer public transport services. All three airports have car-hire facilities.

Scheduled flights from Europe generally stop over, either in Milan, Rome or Naples, from where a Sardinian domestic airline is taken, such as ATI, the sister company of Alitalia, or Alisarda. However, during the summer season, direct flights are made by chartered companies to all three of Sardinia's airports. Scheduled flights operate from all of Italy's main airports all year round. There are also regular internal flights.

Alitalia, British Airways, British Caledonian and Aer Lingus are the major airlines flying to Italy from the UK, while Alitalia and TWA handle most flights from the USA. Most companies, including the internal airlines in Sardinia, offer discounts to students and those under 26.

Ferry

The shortest ferry crossing is from the port of Civitavecchia to Olbia. However, those travelling from Northern Europe, can save on fuel and road tolls by taking the ferry from Genoa. There are crossings from here to Olbia, Porto Torres and Cagliari daily. Those approaching from Southern Italy can make the crossing from Napoli to Cagliari. It is also possible to cross from Sicily, either from Palermo or Trapani, to Cagliari.

Tirrenia Navigazione, the largest ferry company in Italy, operate the greatest choice of crossings. NAV.AR.MA run a service between Livorno and Olbia, while Sardinia Ferries make the crossing between Livorno and Golfo Aranci, which is just to the north of Olbia.

The approximate time each crossing takes is as below.

Genoa-Porto Torres, 12 ½ hours
Genoa-Olbia, 13 hours
Genoa-Cagliari, 21 hours
Livorno-Olbia, 9 hours
Livorno-Golfo Aranci, 10 hours
Civitavecchia-Olbia, 8 hours
Civitavecchia-Cagliari, 13 hours
Napoli-Cagliari, 16 hours
Palermo-Cagliari, 13 ½ hours
Trapani-Cagliari, 11 ½ hours

All ferries carry cars and have cabin accommodation. During the summer season it is necessary to make bookings well in advance for vehicles and cabins. Addresses of ferry booking offices are as follows:

Tirrenia Navigazione:
Cagliari, Agenave, Via Campidano 1
☎ 070 666065
Civitavecchia, Stazione Marittima
☎ 095 316394
Genoa, Stazione Marittima Ponte Colombo
☎ 010 258041
Livorno, Carlo Laviosa, Via Scali d'Azeglio 6
☎ 0586 890632
Napoli, Stazione Marittima molo Angioino
☎ 081 5512181
Olbia, Corso Umberto 17
☎ 0789 24691
Palermo, Calata Marinai d'Italia
☎ 091 333300
Porto Torres, Stazione Marittima
☎ 079 514107
Trapani, Salvo Viaggi di Ruello Antonino, Corso Italia
☎ 0923 23819
UK, Serena Holidays, 40 Kenway Road, London
☎ 373 6548

Sardinia Ferries:
Golfo Aranci
☎ 0789 46780
Genoa, Ponte Caracciolo
☎ 010 253473
Livorno, Nuova Stazione Marittima, Calata Carrara
☎ 0586 881380
Olbia, Corso Umberto 4
☎ 0789 25200
NAV.AR.MA Lines:
Olbia, Corso Umberto 187
☎ 0789 27927
Genoa, Vintiadis Shipping & Travel, Via Ponte Reale 2
☎ 010 205651
Livorno, L.V. Ghianda, Via V. Veneto 24
☎ 0586 890325

Rail
Sardinia can be reached by rail from all major European cities. It takes about 20 hours from London to Genoa, from where the ferry can be taken to Olbia, Porto Torres or Cagliari. The train leaves from London Victoria, changes at Paris, then travels through Turin to Genoa.

The rail system in Sardinia, as in the rest of Italy, is notoriously difficult and prone to strikes. There are only three main lines on the island, that from Olbia to Sassari, another from Olbia to Cagliari, and the last from Cagliari to Sassari. There are branch lines to Porto Torres, Palau, Carbonia and Iglesias. Otherwise, the island is serviced by the Ferrovie Sarde Complementari, which is a narrow gauge line. The main line runs through the centre of Sardinia, from Cagliari to Arbatax. It is a long and tortuous journey, taking about 8 hours, but it offers some remarkable views of the Gennargentu and Barbargia mountains.

Reduced international fares with Interail cards, are available to those under 26, while in Italy itself, a *Carta Verde* can be purchased by young people aged 12 to 26 which gives 30 per cent discount during low season and 20 per cent in high season. Tourists, whose normal place of residence is outside Italy, may purchase a *biglietto turistico libera circolazione*. For a fixed sum, this ticket allows unlimited travel on the Italian state rail network, and does not require a supplement for travel on the *Rapido* (see below). Italian National Tourist Offices (see addresses in the Additional Information sections) will provide details of where tickets may be purchased.

In addition, regular reductions are available for day returns (maximum distance 50km/31 miles), and 3 day returns (maximum distance 250km/155 miles). Discounts are also offered to families, and to parties of between 10 and 20 people. Children under 4, not occupying a seat, travel free, while children under 12 receive a 50 per cent reduction. Those making a round trip of at least 1,000km (620 miles) are also eligible for a special-priced circular ticket. Alternatively, there is a reduced price *chilometrico* ticket, valid for 3,000km (1,860 miles), which can be used by up to 5 people for a maximum of 20 different journeys over a period of 2 months.

Italian trains are classified as below:

Super-rapido (Trans Europa Express). Very fast, luxury class only, supplements payable, booking obligatory.

Rapido Fast inter-city trains. Some are first class only. Supplement charged at about 30 per cent of standard fare, and children pay full supplement. On some trains seat booking is obligatory.

Espresso Long-distance trains between cities, stopping only at major stations.

Diretto Trains stopping at most towns. Look at timetables carefully, as there is often little difference between *Espresso* and *Diretto*.

Locale Stopping at all stations.

By Road

Bus

An extensive bus network covers most areas of Sardinia, with at least one service a day to even the smallest and remotest villages. The main bus company is ARST, Azienda Regionale Sarda Trasporti. There is a private bus company, PANI, which runs services between major centres, and a branch company of the state railway, known as FS. Otherwise, bus services are provided by small local companies. Tickets are sold at the *autostazione*, bus station, or on the bus itself.

Car

The journey by road from London to Rome is over 1,500km (930 miles). It is best to go over the Alps, as passing through the South of France adds a considerable amount to the journey and the roads are very crowded in summer.

Recommended Routes:

1-Boulogne/Calais, Rheims, Lausanne, Great Saint Bernard, Milan, A1.
2-Boulogne, Paris, Bourg en Bresse, M.Blanc, Milan, A1.
3-Ostende, Munich, Innsbruck, Brenner, Milan, A1.

Fuel

All fuel is comparatively expensive in Italy. Diesel, *gasolio*, is somewhat cheaper than petrol, *benzina*, and lead-free petrol, *senza piombo*, is offered at a slight discount. The two grades of fuel available are *benzina normale* and *benzina super*. Lead-free fuel is also offered in two grades, although the *super* variety is not very widely available. Filling stations usually close for lunch between 12.30pm and 3pm, and most are shut on Saturday afternoons and all day Sunday.

Driving Restrictions

When in Sardinia drive on the right and give way to the right. Conventional European road signs are used, and speed limits are 90kph (56mph) outside towns and 50kph (31mph) inside built-up areas. There are heavy on-the-spot fines for speeding, so visitors should take care to observe the speed restriction signs. Sardinia has no motorways or tolls and the roads are generally good. The main artery, which is nearly all dual-carriageway, is the Strada Carlo Felice, which runs from Cagliari to Porto Torres.

Parking is generally not a problem, except in Cagliari and the larger towns. Check when you park your car that you are not in a *zona rimozione* (removal zone) where cars are towed away and are reclaimable at great time and expense, or in a *zona disco* (disc zone), which means cars are only allowed to park for a limited period and must have a disc (available from filling stations), which shows the hour of arrival, displayed in their front window. The authorised parking lots and meters in a town usually charge by the hour, the closer to the centre the higher the tariffs.

Driving Documents and Regulations
All vehicle documents: registration, insurance and driving licence, must be carried at all times with on-the-spot penalties for offenders. Visitors should also carry a translation of their driving licence, available from the AA, RAC or Italian State Tourist Authorities. It is compulsory for front seat passengers to wear seatbelts, and children under 5 must be strapped into a child car seat. It is also compulsory to have a nationality plate and a left-hand wing mirror, and to carry a red warning triangle.

Mopeds
No driving licence is required for mopeds in Italy and anyone over 14 may use them.

Car Hire
Car hire is available at airports, main stations and in most large towns. The major international firms are represented throughout Italy, supplemented by local firms. Most British and American travel agents selling flights or package holidays to Sardinia will be able to offer competitive terms for car hire.

INDEX

Page numbers in **bold** type indicate maps

TRAVEL GUIDE LIST

Airline/Ferry details ....
....
....
....
....

Telephone No. ....

Tickets arrived ☐

Travel insurance ordered ☐

Car hire details ....
....
....

Visas arrived ☐

Passport ☐

Currency ☐

Travellers cheques ☐

Eurocheques ☐

Accommodation address ....
....
....
....

Telephone No. ....

Booking confirmed ☐

Maps required ....
....
....